ISSUES THAT CONCERN YOU

Transgender Rights

Martin Gitlin, *Book Editor*

GREENHAVEN
PUBLISHING

Published in 2018 by Greenhaven Publishing, LLC
353 3rd Avenue, Suite 255, New York, NY 10010

Articles in Greenhaven Publishing anthologies are often edited for length to meet page requirements. In addition, original titles of these works are changed to clearly present the main thesis and to explicitly indicate the author's opinion. Every effort is made to ensure that Greenhaven Publishing accurately reflects the original intent of the authors. Every effort has been made to trace the owners of the copyrighted material.

Library of Congress Cataloging-in-Publication Data

Names: Gitlin, Marty, editor.
Title: Transgender rights / Martin Gitlin, book editor.
Description: First edition. I New York : Greenhaven Publishing, 2018. I
  Series: Issues that concern you I Includes bibliographical references and
  index. I Audience: Grades 9-12.
Identifiers: LCCN 2017031275 I ISBN 9781534502222 (library bound) I 9781534502833
  (paperback)
Subjects: LCSH: Transgender people--Legal status, laws, etc.--United
  States--Juvenile literature. I Sexual minorities--Legal status, laws,
  etc.--United States--Juvenile literature. I Transgender people--Legal
  status, laws, etc.--Juvenile literature.
Classification: LCC KF4754.5 .T73 2017 I DDC 323.3/270973--dc23
LC record available at https://lccn.loc.gov/2017031275

Manufactured in the United States of America

Website: http://greenhavenpublishing.com

CONTENTS

Appendix

When African Americans fought for their civil liberties in the 1950s and 1960s, moral indignation and the belief that the nation must rise up to live out its creed that every person is created equal resulted in triumph. The Civil Rights Act of 1964 and the Voting Rights Act of 1965 ensured that, at least constitutionally, people of color would enjoy the same rights as anyone else.

Today, few disagree that discrimination against any race, gender, or creed should be legally opposed with vigor. But freedom and inclusion have been harder to come by for those in the LGBTQ (lesbian, gay, bisexual, transgender, and queer) community since greater awareness and empathy for their plights first arose in the early 1970s.

Some claim that the difference between LGBTQ citizens and other minorities is that the latter are inescapably and undeniably what they are. They are black or Hispanic or Irish or Jewish or Buddhist. Those who promote or at least accept discrimination against sexual minorities contend that their identities are chosen rather than predetermined. And they further assert that their rights could infringe upon the rights of those with moral or religious objections to what they claim to be a "deviate lifestyle" of their choosing.

The opposing view is that those in the LBGTQ community have no more free choice in their sexual identities than an Asian person has in their ethnicity or a woman has in her gender. They contend that any discrimination leveled upon gay, bisexual, or transgender people weakens the rights of all Americans in that it disallows a select few from the quest of liberty and the pursuit of happiness.

In recent years, the notion that gay people should enjoy equal rights under the law has been greatly accepted in the United States. The Supreme Court ruled in favor of same-sex marriage in 2015, and even a president as conservative as Donald Trump has acknowledged its legality. Controversies such as the refusal of a bureaucrat to issue marriage licenses to gay couples or a business that refused to bake a wedding cake for a gay couple seem likely to arise every so often. But the acceptance of the gay community and the belief that they deserve all the same rights as any other American have evolved greatly since the days of the Stonewall riots, which served as a de facto coming-out party for homosexuals in 1969.

It seems the last sexual minorities left to fight for their rights are transgender people, those who feel they were born into the bodies of the wrong gender and have chosen to undergo sex reassignment surgery. The notion is especially troubling to many, especially those who would consider it an impossible mistake made by an infallible god. The idea of full incorporation of transgender people into American society frightens those with traditional values. But, just like gay people who state categorically that their sexual orientations are not a matter of choice, transgender individuals strongly make the same assertion.

Issues that revolve around transgender freedoms and their supposed infringement upon those who protest those rights on moral or religious grounds have arisen in recent years. The most publicized and contentious has centered on a bill passed in North Carolina demanding that transgender people use only public bathrooms corresponding to the sex identified on their birth certificates. Soon thereafter, the Obama administration directed schools and universities to allow transgender students to use the bathrooms of their choosing, but successor Donald Trump reversed that edict, leaving it up to states and local school districts to decide.

One might downplay the issue in the misconception that the transgender population in the United is too minuscule to make an impact. But a 2016 analysis based on state and federal data showed a rapidly growing number that in 2016 reached 1.4 million, which doubled a previous estimate taken five years earlier. And trends indicate a continuation—younger adults ages eighteen to twenty-four were more likely than older Americans to state that they were transgender.

Issues involving transgender rights indeed are not going

away. And they don't stop at bathroom access. Another debate is whether insurance companies should be forced to pay for gender reassignment surgeries, which has been the case under Obamacare. One would believe that the more conservative Trump administration, which attempted right from its start to rid the country of Obamacare for a myriad of reasons, would not be in favor of insurance companies shelling out millions of dollars for such operations.

A more disturbing problem has been a spate of attacks and even murders of trans people, the number of which rose markedly in 2017 and seemingly tied in with the intolerance often identified with the Trump movement. Eight American trans individuals were victims of hate-crime murders during the first three months of that year. Many have called for a greater awareness of the issue and a nationwide initiative that would help people become educated and empathetic about transgender struggles.

Those struggles include bullying in schools, discrimination in hiring, difficulty in attaining identification for voting purposes, and recent pushes to keep trans people out of the military. But millions who consider violence against transgender people abhorrent also cite religious and moral objections to the concept of sex change. They argue that it is their right to deny service to a trans person on those grounds and refute the charge that it is akin to southerners refusing service to African Americans a half-century ago. Their claim is that trans people are making choices about their gender that most African Americans could never have made about their skin color.

The arguments for and against bathroom access and other issues of civil liberties for transgender people explored in *Issues That Concern You: Transgender Rights* seem destined to rage for quite some time. But as the nation slowly grows more liberal in regard to social issues (after all, who would have thought fifty years ago that gay marriage would become a reality?) it seems that trans people will indeed receive the rights afforded all Americans at some point down the road.

ONE

Religious Beliefs and Transgender Support Can Go Hand-in-Hand

William Gallo and Tina Trinh

> In the following viewpoint, William Gallo and Trina Trinh examine the treatment of trans people by two different Christian churches. Some religious doctrine has been linked to intolerance of transgender people, as well as others in the LBGTQ community. But the authors spotlight North Carolina pastor Chris Ayers, who not only rails against trans discrimination but also has welcomed transgender people into his church. Ayers argues that religious freedom is quite compatible with trans rights, including those that allow them to use public facilities associated with their gender choice. The authors use the contrasting beliefs of another local pastor to show that trans rights still have a long way to go in the religious community, however hopeful Ayers might be that eventually transgender people will be widely accepted by the church. Gallo is a general assignment TV, radio, and web reporter for the Voice of America. Trinh is an international broadcaster at Voice of America.

Chris Ayers is no fire-breathing fundamentalist. But on this particular Sunday in late April, the soft-spoken pastor of Wedgewood Church in Charlotte, North Carolina, is unusually fired up, right from the start of his sermon.

"Does Respect for Transgender People Violate Religious Freedom?" by William Gallo and Tina Trinh, VOA Newsletter, June 2, 2016. Reprinted by permission.

Some places of worship show their support for trans people by displaying rainbow flags. Others are not as welcoming.

"How stupid is HB-2," Ayers says from the pulpit in his welcoming church, emphasizing each of his words slowly and deliberately. "It is not only harmful and discriminatory, it is stupendously stupid."

Ayers is referring to a recently passed law in his state that restricts transgender people to using restrooms and other public facilities that match the gender on their birth certificates rather than the one they identify as.

Many churches in North Carolina support HB-2, saying it reflects their views on gender differences and is necessary to protect women and children from sexual predators.

But not Wedgewood. Over half its members are LGBT. Many are transgender people who say the law stigmatizes them as perverts.

"We are family-type people. We're regular working folks. We have good moral values," says Isley Whitfield, a 52-year-old transgender woman from Charlotte.

"Discrimination Is a Sin"

While LBGT-friendly churches are not uncommon, Wedgewood has made a particular effort to be welcoming. Its front doors are splashed in rainbow colors. A rainbow flag flies outside near a sign that reads, "Discrimination is a sin."

Inside, the traditional restroom signs with the outline of a man and woman lie shattered on a table in the foyer, a symbolic protest to HB-2. They've been replaced by rainbow signs that read "No discrimination."

"Anytime a LGBT person walks through the door of a church, it's really a miracle," says Pastor Ayers. "Because why would anybody try to have a relationship with God after being so rejected by the church in society?"

Support for HB-2

Across the state in Winston Salem, Pastor Ron Baity, who heads the Berean Baptist Church, is also focused on HB-2 and transgender issues.

"We feel like this is a good bill," says Baity, who has organized rallies in support of the law. "It's just common sense that women should use women's restrooms and men should use men's restrooms."

Baity does little to hide his contempt for transgender people. "I think that people who identify as transgender have some very serious problems," he says.

He is part of a conservative Christian movement that views the transgender debate as a defining moment in an effort to defend religious liberty and Biblical ideals.

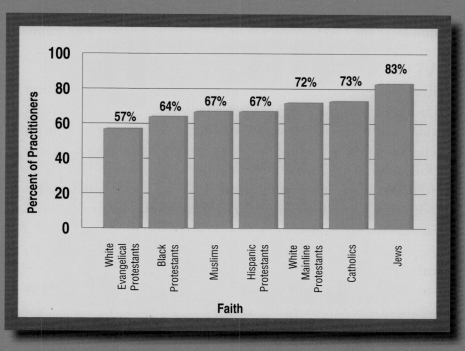

People of faith who support LGBT nondiscrimination protections

Percent of Practitioners

- White Evangelical Protestants: 57%
- Black Protestants: 64%
- Muslims: 67%
- Hispanic Protestants: 67%
- White Mainline Protestants: 72%
- Catholics: 73%
- Jews: 83%

Faith

Preserving Biblical Gender Distinction

Almost a year after the Supreme Court's historic ruling that legalized same sex marriage, the Christian right has seized on the transgender debate as an opportunity to fight back.

Some are pushing ahead with a coordinated initiative that aims to enshrine their values in laws at the state and local level.

Over the past year and a half, 27 states have introduced bills that would restrict transgender bathroom usage (So far, North Carolina is the only state to have passed such a bill).

But for many conservative Christian activists working behind the scenes to advance the legislation, the issue appears to go much deeper than bathroom usage - it's about preserving what they see as the Biblical concept of gender distinction.

"It's frankly absurd to assume that you can change your gender like you can change your clothes, simply because you want to be someone other than your birth sex," says Mathew Staver, the founder of the Liberty Counsel, an evangelical legal defense group.

A Question of Religious Freedom

Staver acknowledges that the Liberty Counsel is one of the driving forces behind the transgender bathroom laws, as well as a wider effort aimed at passing legislation to protect the right of religiously minded people and businesses to deny services to any LGBT individuals.

The Liberty Counsel currently is working on draft legislation and providing other legal consultation in over 22 states, Staver says.

Close to 200 so-called "religious freedom" bills have been introduced by legislators across the country this year alone, according to Rose Saxe, a senior staff attorney at the American Civil Liberties Union.

"I think we're seeing a new sort of argument that basic respect for transgender people violates someone else's religious freedom," Saxe told VOA. "That's not been an argument we've seen until now."

Battle On

Only five states have passed anti-LGBT religious freedom laws so far, but the battle may only beginning.

Brandan Robertson, an author and evangelical activist who supports LGBT rights, predicts conservatives may have short-term success in passing discriminatory laws.

"From a policy perspective, it's a lot easier to propose laws than it is to combat laws," he says. "A lot of us are just now realizing that on the progressive side."

But long term, Robertson says conservative Christians appear to be in trouble, not least of all because opinion polls suggest increasing public support for LBGT rights.

Sensing that pressure, conservatives are spending an enormous amount of money to fight their legal battle on transgender issues, Robertson says.

"Because they know that once we get past this gender debate, then the LGBT rights conversation, in a very real way, is done," he says. "Because then we have L, G, B, and T having equal rights in society."

Ayers, the pastor at Wedgewood Church, is optimistic that his more conservative brothers will eventually come around on the issue, as well.

"I used to be a heterosexual, homophobic, ignorant person," he says." So if God can change me, there's hope, right?

TWO

Transgender People in Public Restrooms: Nothing to Fear but Fear Itself

R. T. Edwins

In the following viewpoint, R. T. (Emma) Edwins exposes the absurdity and ignorance of the frenzy surrounding the so-called "bathroom bill." Much like President Franklin Roosevelt's famed line "The only thing we have to fear is fear itself," Edwins takes the approach that fear, as much as hate, is a powerful driver of discrimination. Using her own experience as a transfeminine person who has visited women's bathrooms frequently without incident, Edwins brings to light the hypocrisy of those who claim that allowing transgender people into their preferred restrooms is dangerous. The more legitimate fear and danger, she writes, is felt by trans people who are forced to use facilities they are uncomfortable in. Edwins is a writer, therapist, and trans activist.

I am a transfeminine person. Many see me simply as a woman or a transwoman, and I use the women's bathroom every single time I need to go to the bathroom in public. I have used the women's bathroom so many times I can't even give you an accurate number. Suffice it to say that it has been at least 100 different times.

"Why There Is Nothing to Be Afraid Of: A Transgender Perspective on Bathroom Laws," by R. T. Edwins, Dara Hoffman-Fox, April 27, 2016. Reprinted by permission.

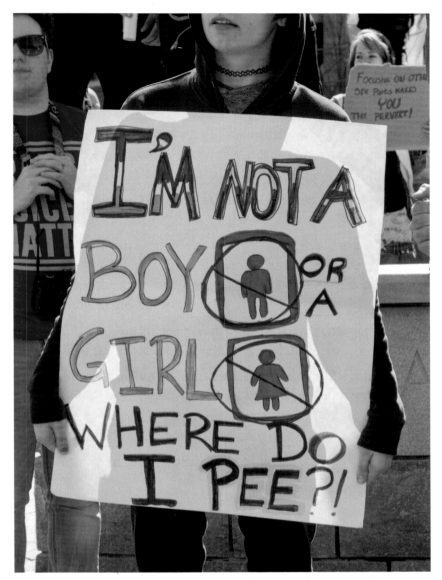

The question of whether transgender people are endangering others by using their preferred public restroom may be rooted in ignorance and fear of the unknown. The issue has been politicized by both the right and the left.

I have never, not even once, thought about how I could utilize this opportunity to attack, harass, or spy on the other women in that bathroom. I have never, not even once, tried to utilize these bathroom visits to satisfy some sort of sexual desire. I am a transfeminine person who is primarily attracted to women and have never once thought about my bathroom visits as anything besides visits to relieve myself.

I have, however, been very scared in the women's bathroom. I have wondered if I would be attacked, harassed or humiliated by the women in there. If a woman in that bathroom looks at me longer than a brief glance my anxiety goes through the roof as I envision her telling me I can't be in there, that I can't stay, or that I am some sort of pervert. I fear for my life and my dignity every time I go into a women's restroom because of the very misinformation that has led to states like North Carolina passing their recent law.

Ignorance Is the Real Danger

Worst still, is the anxiety I feel when considering what it would be like to have to visit the men's room in my current state and appearance. While my fear of being harassed, attacked or humiliated by women is significant, it pales in comparison to the fear I'd feel of experiencing the same at the hands of men. It is not only inappropriate for me to use the men's room, but it is downright dangerous. There has never been any report of a transgender person utilizing their bathroom privileges to harass or attack cisgender people in the bathroom. The opposite scenario is rife with danger, however, and state laws that force transgender individuals into the wrong bathroom only illustrate how dangerous ignorance really is.

We see pictures floating around the internet of extremely masculine transmen with taglines like "coming soon to North Carolina women's bathrooms" and the message is rather clear. It is not appropriate for these individuals to be in these bathrooms and putting a face to the reality of these oppressive laws does illustrate, to a degree, how ridiculous they are. Pictures and taglines, however, are not enough. Visibly seeing what will be happening can change the minds of a few, but we need more than that. We need the humanity behind those pictures. We need the voices, hearts, minds, and souls behind those pictures. It is one thing to see how ludicrous the law is when it forces bearded, muscle-bound men into women's bathrooms, but it is something entirely more to see below the surface to the dehumanizing aspects of the law.

I hope to provide at least a partial account myself but we need more than that. We need more voices speaking out. We need more accounts to be shared. They have to understand the humanity that we have within us so they can stop spreading their hatred and ignorance. I know it is a fight that is unlikely to be won. It is unlikely that people who adhere so ferociously to their dogma and read it in a way that says others are lesser than them will ever truly change, but even if just one person reads my words, or yours for that matter, and has a change of heart then that is a victory.

A Personal Account

My name is Emma, I was born with male genitalia, and I was raised and socialized as a male. I spent the first 28 years of my life using male restrooms and living as a man. I lived as a heterosexual man and when I made the decision to transition from my male life to a transfeminine life, my sexual preferences came with me. I am still very attracted to women. I love women. I find their minds, their hearts, and their bodies lovely to behold and to touch. I still have sex with women, even as I present to the world as a woman, and I use the women's bathroom when in public. In my state of Minnesota the law is somewhat ambiguous on bathroom rights but it often operates on a don't ask, don't tell philosophy. It is most often left up to the individual to decide where they should be going and for many (but not all) transgender individuals that choice is pretty clear. I fall into that category. I look like a woman. I dress like a woman. I sound like a woman. I am seen as and treated as a woman by strangers. I am fortunate that more often than not people do not notice anything off about me and accept me as a woman, which is what I want from those who do not need to know more.

I have used the women's bathroom when other women were in it many times. I have even, as most women do from time to time, stood in line with a group of women waiting for an available stall to alleviate myself. I have chatted with those women in those lines. I have chatted with them as we examined our appearance in the mirror after washing our hands. I have had lovely, completely non-sexual, interactions with women in women's bathrooms countless times and never once did it enter my mind to take advantage of that scenario for my own personal desires, And I'm attracted to women sexually!

Government Overreach

If I, a transfeminine individual who is as attracted to women as most heterosexual men, can have a friendly, non-sexual conversation with a woman I have never met before as we wait in line to pee, then where is this dangerous sexual predator we hear so much about? By all accounts, I fit the exact qualifications for this transgender boogeyman these conservative politicians talk about when they push these laws through state legislatures. I was born male, I cross-dressed as a kid and a teenager, I made the decision to live my life as a woman (or something close to a woman), I am sexually attracted to women, and I use the bathroom with them on a consistent basis... so why haven't I attacked anyone or tried to spy on anyone while in that bathroom?

Maybe, just maybe, it's because this boogeyman these politicians try to force down our throats doesn't actually exist. Maybe, just maybe, we transgender individuals are in the bathroom just because we need to go to the bathroom. Maybe, just maybe, we don't have any ulterior motives for entering that most sacred of places where women and children go to pee. Maybe, and this could be a stretch for some I'll admit, I go into the women's bathroom to pee simply because I am a woman and I have the right to decide I'm a woman, and I have the right to know where the appropriate place is for me to pee.

Conservatives push and push again for government deregulation. They say government overreach is a true struggle of our time. They advocate deregulating our economy, our gun laws, our tax code, and our social services. They say that big government doesn't have the right to enter our homes and tell us how to live because we are Americans, and America is the land of the free. They talk about how we all have the ability to pull ourselves up by our bootstraps and that individual work and choices is what makes our country great, except when it comes to people like me.

When it comes to me, a person they refuse to understand and barely acknowledge even exists, it is not only appropriate for the government to step in and regulate where I can use the bathroom and where I can't (the most personal of personal freedoms, I'd argue) but it is mandatory that they do. They have to "protect" our free society from the menace of those who don't fit into their gender binary and their heterosexual worldview because they are different, and different, of course, means dangerous. Then, and only then, is it okay for government overreach to be tolerated, accepted, and enacted into law.

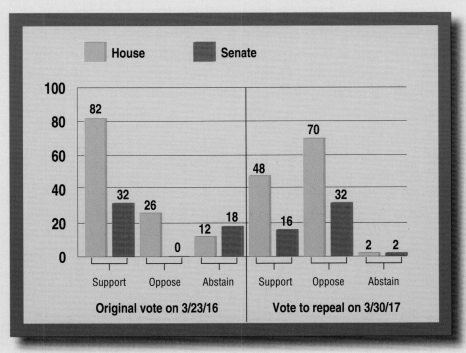

How North Carolina state legislators voted on HB-2 when introduced on March 23, 2016, and a bill for its repeal on March 30, 2017

Sources: CNN and NBC

I cannot adequately express into words how disheartening this is as a transgender individual. I cannot put into words for you to understand the sick feeling I get in the pit of my stomach as I watch these politicians sign their bills into law with grins on their faces, like they are proud of their bigotry, hatred, and fear. I live in a state where one of these bills is being pushed through our legislature by these same conservative efforts to regulate where I pee. Luckily our governor has already said he will veto it, but he won't be the governor forever and there is no guarantee the next governor or the next legislature won't succeed where this attempt to make oppression the law of our state has failed. Multiple states have already turned these oppressive bills into laws.

I feel so powerless. So broken, and misunderstood, and defeated when I see what happened in North Carolina. I just need to pee. We all just need to pee. We aren't a menace. We aren't a danger. We've been here all along, peeing right next to you without you even knowing. We've been here forever, really. Transgender isn't a new thing, even if the term is new. We are humans. We have feelings, hearts, minds, and fears, and right now, we are afraid of the conservative pushback to transgender visibility. We don't deserve to be ignored, but we absolutely don't deserve to be oppressed further than we already are as a consequence of our visibility. Please don't buy into their boogeyman antics. Just because you may think we are different, doesn't mean we are dangerous. We are just people… just like you.

THREE

Obama's Rebuke of the Bathroom Bill Did Not Go Far Enough

Tom Carter

In the following viewpoint, Tom Carter lambastes North Carolina's House Bill 2, which seeks to force trans people to use public restrooms corresponding to their birth gender. He also criticizes then-President Obama's condemnation of the bill for not going far enough. The author claims that HB2 also kills local laws that protect North Carolina citizens based on sexual orientation, race, religion, gender, and national origin. He states that the Obama rebuke of the bill merely targets public school districts that would not allow transgender people to use the restrooms that choose, but should have been more inclusive. Carter is a contributor to World Socialist website.

The Obama administration on May 13 issued a letter requiring all public school districts in the country to permit transgender students to use the bathroom of their choice. This decision marks an escalation of the ongoing political and media controversy over a North Carolina statute that would require transgender individuals to use the bathroom that corresponds to their sex as stipulated on their birth certificate.

The letter, issued jointly by the Department of Education and the Department of Justice, included guidelines purportedly

"The Controversy In The US Over Transgender Access To Public Bathrooms," by Tom Carter, World Socialist Web Site, May 18, 2016. Reprinted by permission.

North Carolina's House Bill 2 is not only a "bathroom bill." The law also promotes discriminatory practices in other areas.

designed to ensure that "transgender students enjoy a supportive and nondiscriminatory school environment." Schools that fail to follow the guidelines can face a cutoff of federal funding.

North Carolina's House Bill 2 (HB2), passed by the state legislature and signed into law by Republican Governor Pat McCrory in March, overturns a Charlotte City Council decision to allow transgender individuals to use the bathroom of the gender with which they identify. HB2 is reactionary and must be opposed, together with the rest of the recent efforts by Republican-controlled state legislatures to pass laws invoking "religious liberty" to whip up bigotry and codify intolerance against gay and transgender people.

That being said, the presentation by the Obama administration and much of the media of bathroom access for transgender people as the single most critical issue of the day is grossly disproportionate to its intrinsic significance and has the character of a political diversion. The American people, and the people of the entire world, are confronting issues of the most immense and urgent import—the growing danger of world war, the growth of poverty and inequality, the militarization of society and drive toward dictatorship. These issues are either being buried or trivialized in the US election campaign.

An Assault on Our Democratic Rights

It is significant that the Obama administration is waging its campaign over only one of the many reactionary provisions of the North Carolina statute. Under the guise of upholding "religious liberty," HB2 goes much further, nullifying local laws protecting residents against discrimination based not only on sexual orientation, but also on race, religion, color, national origin, gender or physical handicap. The North Carolina law also includes a provision banning any local minimum wage—a fact left out of virtually all media accounts of the controversy.

HB2 is itself only one of a number of similar anti-democratic and discriminatory laws targeting gay and transgender individuals that have been recently introduced or passed throughout the country, including in Georgia, Indiana, Arkansas, Kentucky, West Virginia, South Dakota and other states. These laws take as their starting point the Supreme Court's reactionary 2014 *Hobby Lobby* decision upholding the "religious liberty" of corporations to refuse to pay for birth control for employees.

Perhaps the most egregious of these measures is a Mississippi bill that explicitly allows specific forms of discrimination, such as denying contracts and scholarships, withholding state benefits, denying marriage and other licenses and certifications, withholding diplomas and grades, imposing tax penalties, and carrying out workplace retaliation, including termination. The Mississippi law is not limited to gay or transgender people, but also codifies discrimination against anyone who has "sexual relations" outside of heterosexual marriage. In more than half of US states, it is currently legal for an employer to fire an employee for being gay.

These laws will have a punitive impact on gays and other targeted individuals. But their implications are far broader. They are part of an assault on the democratic rights of the population as a whole. They are bound up with a relentless attack on the separation of church and state, a keystone of the US Constitution's Bill of Rights.

This offensive is being waged on the basis of a false presentation of religious liberty that turns an important democratic principle into its opposite, i.e., the "right" of an organization or business, citing religious belief, to deny its employees access to birth control and refuse to serve gays. If an employer can fire an employee for being gay, there is no reason in principle why he cannot fire someone for being an atheist, or black, or Jewish.

Political Maneuverings

These reactionary laws are not a response to popular pressure. On the contrary, recent years have seen a marked decline in these forms of intolerance within the population. It is, rather, the response of the most rabidly reactionary and fascistic elements within the ruling elite and the political establishment to the deepening crisis of American capitalism, together with the growth of social opposition and anti-capitalist sentiment. Centered in the Republican Party, this element is seeking to appeal to the most backward conceptions and whip up the most reactionary social forces.

For their part, the Obama administration and the Democratic Party are giving the issue of what bathrooms transgender individuals should use a vastly disproportionate level of political attention. A relative handful of people are directly affected in a country where the democratic rights of hundreds of millions of people are under ferocious assault by both capitalist parties.

There is an immense element of political and electoral calculation and cynicism on both sides of this controversy. In an election dominated by mass anger over economic inequality and the control of the political system by Wall Street, there is a desire by both parties to change the subject. The Republicans are seeking to mobilize their base among more backward, disoriented and economically depressed middle class layers. The Democrats are seeking to appeal to layers of the more privileged upper-middle class

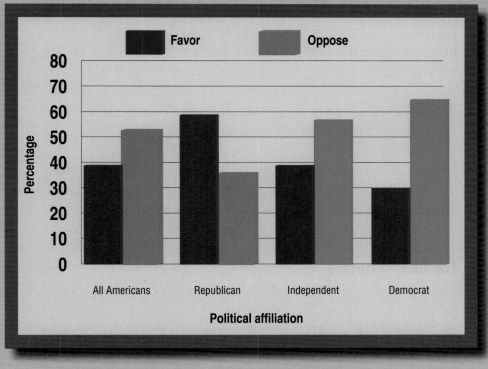

Percentage of Americans who oppose laws requiring transgender individuals to use bathrooms that correspond to their sex at birth, by political affiliation

Source: PRRI

that have made various issues of identity—race, gender, sexual orientation—their obsessive focus.

In a speech on May 9, Attorney General Loretta Lynch compared the campaign against the North Carolina statute to the struggles of the civil rights movement of the 1950s and 1960s against Jim Crow segregation. "This is not the first time that we have seen discriminatory responses to historic moments of progress for our nation," she said. "We saw it in the Jim Crow laws that followed the Emancipation Proclamation. We saw it in fierce and widespread resistance to *Brown v. Board of Education*"—a reference to the 1954 Supreme Court ruling abolishing racial segregation in public schools.

The Obama administration's attempt to cloak itself in the legacy of the civil rights movement is as fraudulent as the historical comparison is inappropriate. The Democrats have barely lifted a finger in response to the Supreme Court's reactionary 2013 ruling gutting the 1965 Voting Rights Act, which was arguably the most significant reform that resulted from the struggles of that period. Not a single bill has been introduced on the floor of either house of Congress to revive the enforcement provisions that were struck down by the Supreme Court. The Democrats' capitulation has emboldened Republican-controlled state governments around the country, which have shifted onto the offensive, to enact anti-democratic voter ID requirements and other measures that discriminate against working class, poor, and minority voters.

Identity Politics

The comparison of the question of bathroom access for transgender individuals to the struggle against Jim Crow also ignores the much more complicated and sensitive cultural and legal questions involved. For example, which communal showers it is best for transgender high school students to use, and on what sports teams they should compete, are questions that cannot necessarily be resolved with simple answers. One expects that with the passage of time, architecture and customs will adapt. The Obama administration's heavy-handed and disproportionate campaign over this issue ends up trivializing struggles over issues of much broader democratic significance.

The posturing of the Obama administration and the Democratic Party with respect to the North Carolina "bathroom bill" reflects their strategy of using identity politics to provide a cover for their own right-wing and anti-democratic policies. Identity politics, whether based on race, gender or sexual orientation, have been promoted for decades and become central components of the ideological and political arsenal of the ruling elite.

Far from promoting the interests of the vast majority of minorities or women, these policies have coincided with a sustained assault on the living standards of all sections of the working class and a colossal growth of social inequality. The Democratic Party has presided, no less than the Republicans, over this offensive against the working class.

Obama, touted by the proponents of identity politics as the first African-American president, has overseen the biggest increase in social inequality in American history. The frontrunner for the Democratic presidential nomination in 2016, Hillary Clinton, who is marketing herself as potentially the first female president, as first lady supported her husband's termination of federal welfare benefits for the poor and the adoption of reactionary law-and-order legislation that has resulted in the imprisonment of huge numbers of poor and minority youth for non-violent crimes.

Under Democratic and Republican administrations alike—from Clinton to Bush to Obama—civil liberties have been progressively shredded. The Obama administration, in particular, will be remembered for the militarization of police, the assertion of the president's power to assassinate anyone in the world, amnesty for torturers and financial criminals, rampant corruption and criminality, a vast police state spying operation against the population, and the persecution of whistleblowers.

Precisely on issues that are of particular concern to women, such as birth control and abortion rights, Obama and the Democratic Party have carried out one cowardly retreat and capitulation to churches and the religious right after another, providing the right-wing majority on the Supreme Court with ammunition to uphold the "right" of businesses and other organizations to discriminate on religious grounds.

Those middle-class "left" individuals and tendencies that are falling into line behind the Obama administration's political maneuver on the issue of transgender bathroom access are taking their obsessive fixation on issues of sex and gender to new heights of absurdity. The essential political function of all forms of identity politics is to obscure the basic class issues in society and politics and obstruct the political unification of the working class on a revolutionary socialist basis. The attempt to make the issue of transgender bathroom access the overriding issue before the American people will not be the end of such efforts.

FOUR

The Government and Insurance Companies Should Help Cover Gender Reassignment Surgery

Anna Gorman

> In the following viewpoint, Anna Gorman examines the challenges faced by trans people who opt for gender reassignment surgery. Under the Affordable Care Act (ACA), the procedure was covered through health insurance, a boon for many in the trans community. Gorman uses the case of Devin Payne, a trans woman who underwent gender reassignment surgery thanks to insurance and subsidies, to shed light on discriminatory practices that kept so many trans people from receiving the surgeries they needed. Since this article was written, however, Obamacare has been threatened by succeeding president Donald Trump and Republican lawmakers. Gorman is senior correspondent for Kaiser Health News and a former *Los Angeles Times* journalist.

Devin Payne had gone years without health insurance – having little need and not much money to pay for it.

Then Payne, who had a wife and four children, realized she could no longer live as a man.

In her early 40s, she changed her name, began wearing long skirts and grew out her sandy blond hair. And she started taking female hormones, which caused her breasts to develop and the muscle mass on her 6-foot one-inch frame to shrink.

The next step was gender reassignment surgery. For that, Payne, who is now 44, said she needed health coverage. "It is not a simple, easy, magical surgery," said Payne, a photographer who lives in Palm Springs. "Trying to do this without insurance is a big risk. Things can go wrong ... not having the money to pay for it would be awful."

Payne learned in the fall that she might qualify for subsidies through the state's new insurance marketplace, Covered California, because her income fell under the limit of $46,000 a year. She eagerly signed up in March for a Blue Shield plan for about $230 a month, and began making preparations for the surgery that would change her life.

A "Pre-existing Condition"

Among the less-talked-about implications of the Affordable Care Act is the relief it is providing to many transgender people, many of whom are low-income and who have struggled to obtain health coverage.

Getting jobs that offer insurance often has been difficult for transgender people and the cost of purchasing plans on the private market can be prohibitive. Some have been denied policies altogether after being diagnosed with "gender identity disorder," often considered a pre-existing condition.

Without insurance, many people were unable to afford the hormones, surgeries and counseling needed to complete their transition. Nor would they have been covered in the event of surgical complications, which can include infections.

"We are still dependent on insurance and the medical community for us to be able to live authentically," said Aydin Kennedy,

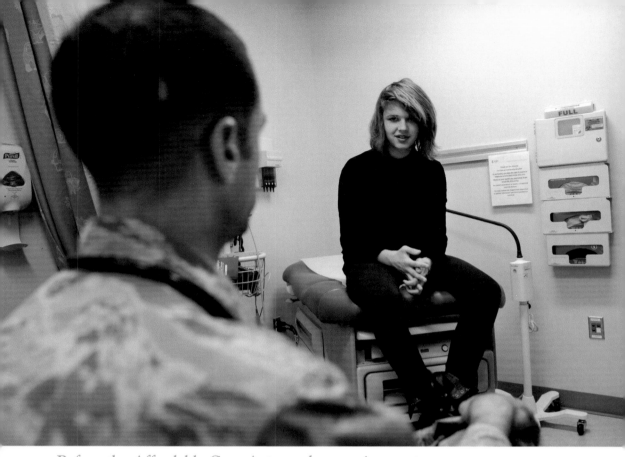

Before the Affordable Care Act, gender reassignment surgery and hormone therapy were unattainable for those without the resources to pay for them.

coordinator of the transgender health program at St. John's Well Child and Family Center in Los Angeles.

Now, federal law prohibits health insurance companies from discriminating against transgender people, and it bars insurers from denying coverage based on pre-existing conditions. That makes it possible for more transgender people to purchase private plans. And in states that expanded their Medicaid programs, those with low incomes may get free coverage.

The federal anti-discrimination regulations have yet to be written, but California insurance regulators have said that companies must treat transgender patients the same as other patients. For example, if plans cover hormones for post-menopausal women, they must also cover them for transgender

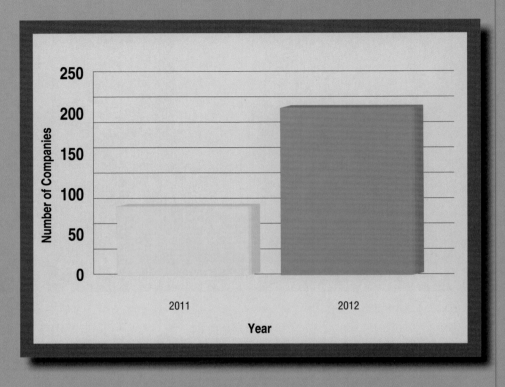

Source: Human Rights Campaign

women. Medicare, the program for the elderly and disabled, lifted its ban on covering sex reassignment surgery earlier this year.

"The law and policy are on a transgender person's side for the first time," said Anand Kalra, program administrator at the Oakland-based Transgender Law Center.

Conservative and religious groups oppose using government funds for transgender surgeries, questioning whether they are medically necessary, ethical or effective.

"We would oppose sex change operations all together," said Peter Sprigg, senior fellow at the Family Research Council in Washington, D.C. "But as a public policy issue, we would feel particularly strongly that taxpayers shouldn't be asked to pay for it."

A few obstacles remain for transgender patients. Not many doctors specialize in transgender care. And while the law opens the door to insurance coverage, insurers can set conditions and don't automatically approve payment.

"Insurance companies are making up their own rules as they go along," said Kalra of the Transgender Law Center.

"Feeling Complete"

Growing up in Kansas, Payne remembers trying on her mother's clothes and dressing as a girl every year for Halloween. She dreamt of having another life after this one, as a girl. But Payne said she mostly suppressed her feelings and tried to live up to the expectations for a male.

"I put it out of my head," she said.

She married a woman she met at work and they had four children, now ages 7 to 22. But she never felt comfortable in the traditional role of father and provider.

"I was just horrible at it because it wasn't who I was," she said. So Payne became the primary caretaker, playing the "mommy role" as she worked from home doing software development for pharmaceutical companies.

She felt increasingly anxious, and in late 2012, a therapist helped her to realize that she was meant to live as a woman. Payne said her entire outlook on life changed when she started taking female hormones.

"All my anxiety and all of the bad things that I felt inside were just completely washed away," she said.

Payne told her wife, who was upset. She told Payne: I married a man, not a woman — but she also admitted that she wasn't entirely surprised. With mixed feelings, Payne's wife stayed in the marriage, and the family moved from Kansas to California, in part so Payne could be more comfortable living as a transgender woman. They rented a small house in a middle class neighborhood on the outskirts of Palm Springs and sent their children to the public school.

Late last year, Payne's wife, who had battled alcoholism for years, died of liver disease.

Payne said the children worried how people would react to her transition, but she said they soon realized it wasn't as big of a deal as they had feared. When Payne brought birthday cupcakes to her 7-year-old daughter's classroom last year, the children asked if she was a girl or a boy. After Payne told them she was a girl, "they just wanted their cupcakes."

In California, Payne found transgender friends and became an advocate within the community. "You find out that there is a whole world of people out there," said Payne, who wears little makeup or jewelry and calls herself a "T-shirt and skirt kind of a girl."

Payne was ready for the surgery. She started calling the approved providers in Blue Shield's preferred provider network. But they were booked up for months, or years. She felt she couldn't wait — she wanted to do the surgery while her children were on summer vacation so they could go to her parents' house in Kansas as she recovered. She found an out-of-network doctor in Palo Alto who would do the surgery about a month later.

"The time was right and I wanted to get it done," she said.

Her Blue Shield policy said that gender reassignment surgery – which uses existing tissue to construct female genitalia — could be covered if patients met certain guidelines. For example, she had to be diagnosed with gender identity disorder and have an "expressed desire" to live as a member of the opposite sex.

By the scheduled date, Blue Shield had authorized the operation but hadn't determined exactly how much it would pay for an out-of-network provider. Payne got a cashier's check for nearly all her savings, $27,000, to pay the doctor, hoping her insurance plan would reimburse most of it. She worried about all the other expenses too, including the hospital stay, lab work and anesthesiology services.

The day of the surgery at Sequoia Hospital in Redwood City, Payne said she remembers being wheeled in to the operating room and feeling very calm. When she woke up, with oxygen still attached and wearing her hospital gown, a friend told her that the surgery had gone well, without any immediate complications.

Later that day, she had just enough energy to type a few words on her Facebook profile: "Feeling complete."

Grateful for Coverage

On a boiling afternoon in early July, about six weeks after the operation, Payne and her friends sat outside on the patio next to a pool. Misters sprayed above them, and Payne's cat and two dogs wandered beneath their feet.

Payne said she did suffer a few complications later – some swelling and an infection — but she recovered with medication and support from friends.

She is still trying to figure out how much she has to pay out-of-pocket for the surgery and hospital stay — and how much of that her insurance plan will reimburse. Payne said she believes the lab work, pathology, anesthesiology services and follow-up doctor's visits were all covered. But recently she got a statement saying she was on the hook for $17,000 of the total cost of the surgery.

Payne believes that the government and insurance companies should help cover such operations. The population of transgender patients who want surgery is small, and she said they are less likely to suffer mental health problems once they have it.

Payne said she will be grateful for whatever coverage she can receive. Her friend Jenny Taylor, who is staying with her during the recovery, has had an even harder time with her insurance.

An outgoing transgender woman who laughs easily and wears colorful outfits and painted nails, Taylor purchased a policy through the insurance exchange in Tennessee. But she soon learned her doctor wasn't in the plan's network and that she had to pay cash for everything, with no hope of reimbursement.

"My insurance, even though I finally got it, was useless," she said.

The policy also wouldn't pay for her hormones. A pharmacist told her the medication was for women – and her identification still listed her as a male. Taylor recently moved to Palm Springs and said she now plans to apply for insurance through Covered California.

"I was really frustrated," she said. "We're just trying to be ourselves, at the end of the day."

Payne agreed, saying she finally feels like her body matches what she knows to be true – that she is a woman. "It seems more natural," she said.

Updates

January 2015

About seven months after her gender reassignment surgery, Devin Payne said she is thankful she was able to have the operation and to have some of it covered by insurance.

In the end, Payne estimates that she paid about $18,000 – about a third of the total cost. Her insurer, Blue Shield of California, picked up the rest.

"The insurance was for me a safety net," she said. She knew that if there were complications, she wouldn't go bankrupt.

Payne said she is looking into whether she can get the insurance company to cover more of the expenses. She believes that fighting the insurance company could help other transgender men and women who want to have surgery in the future.

In December, Payne had some revisions made by her surgeon and said she is feeling better every day. Meanwhile, she is spending time with friends and working as a photographer. Her children, who were staying with her parents as she recovered, are back home with her in Palm Springs.

"I have a house full of kids again," she said. "Everything is kind of back to normal."

More than a year after her gender reassignment surgery, Devin Payne said she is in good health and has settled into her new body.

"My life makes more sense this way," she said. "Before, I felt awkward and out of place. Now, I feel comfortable with my body, in my body and with the way I look."

In the end, Payne said, being able to get the surgery through her Covered California plan "turned out to be a pretty good deal." The insurance company picked up most of the costs, she said. "It was fair and affordable."

Payne said she feels like her story isn't so novel anymore, because more and more transgender people are able to get their private insurance and Medicare to cover their operations. "The great thing is that there is so much visibility," she said.

Now 44, Payne said she is focusing on raising her children. They are also healthy, and have only used the insurance plan for routine physicals and immunizations, she said.

The family is planning to embark on a new adventure – a move out of state. Payne said she feels confident that wherever they end up, she will not have to worry about being denied insurance.

"With Obamacare, I know I will get insurance … and I know it's going to be affordable," she said. "It is not as big of an issue."

FIVE

The Sporting World Is Unfair to Transgender Athletes

Katharina Lindner

In the following viewpoint, Katharina Lindner argues that a decision by the International Olympic Committee to allow transgender athletes to compete without having undergone gender reassignment surgery could have major implications. Lindner questions whether female athletes will be at a competitive disadvantage competing against bigger, stronger, faster men who identify as women, but have not undergone the procedure. She further questions the IOC's plan to use hormone levels for purposes of sex testing in its drive for inclusion of trans peoples. Lindner explains her views through her knowledge of biological differences between the sexes and the methods of testing involved. Lindner is a lecturer at the University of Stirling in the UK and is a member of the Centre for Gender and Feminist Studies.

It hasn't always been plain sailing for women in sport. With a history marked by division and discrimination, it looks like things could be about to get a whole lot more complicated for female athletes, after the International Olympic Committee announced changes to its transgender policy.

Trans male wrestler Mack Beggs was forced by state law to compete against girls because he was assigned that gender at birth.

Transgender athletes will now be allowed to compete in the Olympics without having to undergo sex reassignment surgery. Which is possibly set to impact women's sport more than men's. Achieving eligibility to compete in male competition is now easy - you just have to say you are male. Whereas eligibility to compete in female competition is subject to a number of tests for hormone levels.

For some, this step away from surgical requirements was enthusiastically welcomed and considered an important milestone towards greater equality and inclusion in the sporting world. But there were also much more critical responses. These included

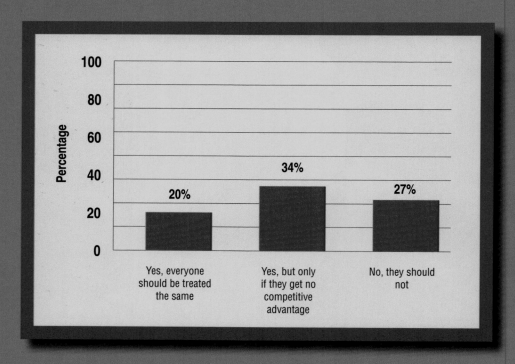

Percentage of people polled who think athletes that have undergone gender reassignment should be allowed to compete as their new gender

Source: YouGov.com

concerns around the possible impact on the integrity and fairness of competition. And fears that women in particular would be even further disadvantaged within sport than they already are.

Questions of Biology

The *Times* columnist Janice Turner said the new policy was "great news – unless you are a woman athlete" and that "trans athletes are unfair to women." Her concerns are based on assumptions that male-to-female trans athletes will always have a biological advantage in terms of size, muscle mass and lung capacity.

For Turner, the new policy, while seemingly more inclusive, is bound to be exploited by "medal-hungry male athletes in unscrupulous nations." One example Turner mentions is the case of the Iranian women's football national team, which allegedly includes eight men who are currently "awaiting sex change operations."

But female athletes, especially the most talented ones have long had their gender called into question. In 2009 Caster Semenya the female South-African middle distance runner, was forced to undergo sex testing after her 800-metre victory at the 2009 World Championships was considered too fast for a woman. Which is another example that demonstrates how debates about unfair competitive advantage intersect with concerns around "real" female athletes' marginalisation.

Testing Time

The move towards using hormone levels for purposes of sex testing and in transgender inclusion policies is useful. It is hormones, especially androgens such as testosterone – and not reproductive organs – that are linked to muscle mass, speed and strength and competitive advantage.

But here's where the trouble starts. The "female" sex hormone oestrogen is generally found in higher levels in women. And men tend to have higher levels of androgens like testosterone. But both oestrogens and androgens are also found in men and women. Making any cutoff point, such as trans women requiring a consistent testosterone level below 10 nmol/L – the level set by the IOC – is pretty arbitrary, and ultimately useless.

The IOC's use of hormone levels to measure or test sex has replaced earlier "gender verification" practices. These previously involved asking female athletes to drop their underwear, but eventually a less humiliating method was found: checking swabs of cheek tissue for chromosomes, as "proof" of an athlete's sex. Women have vaginas, ovaries and XX chromosomes, and men have penises and XY chromosomes. Sounds simple right? Wrong.

The move away from using reproductive organs or chromosomes was linked to scientific evidence which showed that "nature" is a lot messier than we think. There is no neat and clear distinction between "male" and "female" – and no way of "measuring" or "testing" sex based on reproductive organs or chromosomes alone.

There are much greater variations of sex chromosomes than simply XX and XY, including XXY, XXXY, XXXXY, XXYY, XXXYY. And chromosomes themselves also don't have a direct impact on the body's physical characteristics – they only do so when combined with certain hormones. Then add intersex people, discrepancies between internal and external sex organs and mismatches between genitals and chromosomal sex into the mix - and you've got a whole lot of complication. As was the case with Semenya.

Facing the Future

On the whole, the physical differences among men and among women are bigger than the differences between men and women. Semenya might have higher testosterone levels and greater muscles mass than the "average woman" - but the same might also be said about Usain Bolt when compared to the "average man."

The IOC's new policy is then, perhaps, the best we can do, at the moment, given that sport is a gender-segregated context.

Removing the need for transgender athletes to undergo sex reassignment surgery is a welcome acknowledgement that bodies don't come in neatly defined categories. And using hormone levels as a measure seems a pragmatic compromise. That said, the increasingly popular sport of roller derby puts the rest of the sporting world to shame with its move away from gender-segregation and its refreshingly progressive policies for trans people, genderqueer and nonbinary inclusion.

Assuming mainstream sport will remain gender-segregated for the time being, what is needed then is education to prevent prejudice, exclusion and knee-jerk reactions by sports policy makers, governing bodies and the media. And continuing conversations between those promoting equality for women in sport and advocates for transgender inclusion are vital to iron out any unproductive misconceptions on both sides.

SIX

Hate Crime Laws Must Go Further to Protect Transgender Individuals

Victoria Law

> In the following viewpoint, Victoria Law argues that the spate of anti trans violence in recent years has proven that the laws enacted against hate crimes do not adequately protect trans people. Law cites many attacks against transgender people from 2008 to the time the article was written in 2011 in offering her concerns that hate crime legislation must go further in specifically targeting violence against individuals in the trans community. And finally, she argues, the public must be educated about trans issues so that discrimination and violence are avoided altogether. Law is a freelance journalist who focuses on the intersections of incarceration, gender, and resistance, and is the author of *Resistance Behind Bars: The Struggles of Incarcerated Women.*

On the morning of June 5, 2011, a 23-year-old African-American transgender woman, Chrishaun McDonald, and her friends were walking down Lake Street in Minneapolis. As they passed Schooner Tavern, Dean Schmitz, a 47-year-old white man, began shouting racial slurs at McDonald, asking, "Did you think you were going to rape somebody in those girl clothes?" Schmitz and two other bar patrons then attacked McDonald.

"Anti-Transgender Violence: How Hate-Crime Laws Have Failed," by Victoria Law, Truthout, September 18, 2011. ©Truthout.org. Reprinted by permission.

Trans people are more likely to face harrassment and violence, including murder. Many believe such actions should be classified as hate crimes.

During the attack, glass was smashed into McDonald's face and Schmitz was killed. McDonald was arrested and charged with second-degree murder.

The details of what happened are still not clear. However, considering the widespread discrimination, harassment and violence that transgender people face every day in the United States, McDonald and her friends had ample reason to fear that Schmitz's attack could lead to serious injury, if not death. A recent report by the National Coalition of Anti-Violence Programs found that 50 percent of LGBT (lesbian, gay, bisexual and transgender) murders in 2009 and 44 percent of LGBT murders in 2010 were of transgender women. This year does not seem to be a safer year for transgender people either:

- In January 2011, in Minneapolis, a transgender woman named Krissy Bates was strangled and then stabbed to death by her new boyfriend.

- In February, the body of an African-American transgender woman, Tyra Trent, was found in an abandoned house in Baltimore.

- In April, Chrissy Lee Polis, a 22-year-old white transgender woman, was brutally beaten by two black teenage girls at a McDonald's in Baltimore, Maryland. The vicious attack made news only because an employee filmed and posted it online. The video captured not only the assault, but the lack of intervention from both employees and other patrons. While the attack on Polis may not have been fully motivated by her gender identity, bystanders' unwillingness to intervene was.

Given these recent attacks and the lack of public outcry, or even sympathy, one can understand why McDonald and her friends feared for her life when attacked that morning.

Trying to Legislate Away Hate

Following the attack on Polis, Equality Maryland, an LGBTQ (lesbian, gay, bisexual, transgender and queer) advocacy group, called on the state attorney general to prosecute the assault as a hate crime based on gender identity.

Some anti-violence advocates, however, argue that hate-crime charges are more likely to be sought by the state in cases where black people have hurt white people, further bolstering the disproportionate number of black people in prison. The attack on Polis originally received such widespread attention in part because of the racial dynamics: the attackers are black and Polis is white, prompting the state's attorney to consider hate-crime charges based on race. In Minneapolis, the Trans Youth Support Network (TYSN) noted that, while one of McDonald's assailants had a swastika tattoo and the attack was clearly motivated by both her race and gender identity, the state is not prosecuting the white woman who smashed glass into her face.[1]

Hate-crime legislation also has not stopped the endemic violence against transgender people. Just weeks after Obama signed the Matthew Shepard and James Byrd Hate Crimes Prevention Act, the country's first gender identity and sexual orientation inclusive hate-crimes bill, two young queer people of color were murdered, one in Maryland, the other in Puerto Rico. In the wake of both the Act and the killings, two LGBT anti-violence organizations, the Audre Lorde Project in New York and Communities United Against Violence in San Francisco, issued a statement pointing out that the bill provides no funding or resources to actually prevent violence. Instead, it reaffirms the idea that safety is realized by more police and more imprisonment, allocating five million dollars to expand the powers of local police and the FBI to investigate and prosecute hate violence, while ignoring the violence perpetrated by law enforcement. Despite hate-crime laws, the combination of transphobia and racism makes transgender people of color more likely to encounter police indifference when reporting violence, and three times more likely to experience hate violence from police than white transgender or non-transgender people of color. The National Coalition of Anti-Violence Programs found that 8 percent of hate violence against transgender people of color in 2010 was committed by police officers.

Transgender people often face severe discrimination, resulting in a lack of resources and opportunities and placing them further at risk for violence. Although 14 states and Washington, DC, have some measure of legal protection for transgender people against discrimination, this legislation has not decreased actual discrimination: Although New York City has had anti-discrimination laws since 2002, a 2007 study by the Sylvia Rivera Law Project, a legal aid organization for transgender, transsexual, intersex and other gender non-conforming people in New York City, found that transgender and gender non-conforming people suffer pervasive discrimination in housing, employment, health care, education,

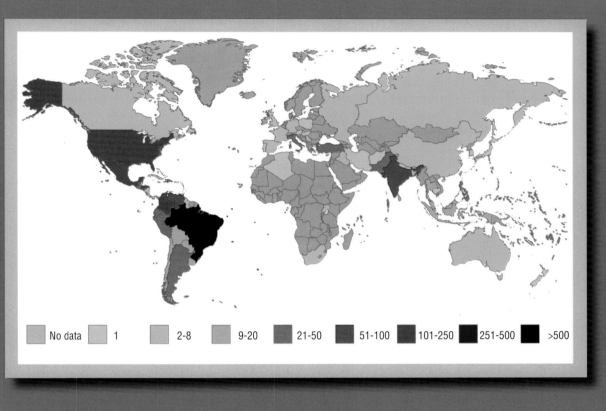

Reported number of murders of trans people per country, from January 2008 to December 2015

No data | 1 | 2-8 | 9-20 | 21-50 | 51-100 | 101-250 | 251-500 | >500

Source: Galop

public benefits and social services. This lack of access pushes a disproportionate number of transgender youth and adults into criminalized means of survival, such as sex work, drug sales or theft. The study also found that, because of entrenched social stigma, transgender people encounter pervasive violence and physical brutality from family members, community members and police. Widespread discrimination and violence often prevent transgender people from accessing shelters, foster care, Medicaid, public entitlements and social safety nets, which would enable them to survive without turning to illegal activities. As a result, transgender people are disproportionately poor, homeless, criminalized and imprisoned.

New York City is not the only anomaly. Although San Francisco has had anti-discrimination laws since 1994, a 1997 survey by its Department of Public Health found that more than 30 percent of transgender women had spent time behind bars during the preceding 12 months. While in prison, transgender people experience further violence, from being placed in prisons according to their birth-assigned genders and/or genitalia, to rampant verbal, physical and sexual violence from both staff and other prisoners. TYSN Director Katie Burgess noted that McDonald was placed in solitary confinement in a men's jail because of her gender identity.

Even when transgender people are offered alternatives to incarceration, they encounter difficulties finding facilities willing to recognize and respect their gender identity. In 2008, Sabire Wilson, a transgender woman arrested for drug possession in New York City, accepted a plea bargain to enter a drug treatment center instead of prison. She chose Phoenix House because it purported to be gay and lesbian friendly. However, because Wilson's assigned gender is male, the admissions counselor agreed to admit her so long as she used the male dormitories and bathroom. Wilson agreed as long as staff allowed her to dress and present herself as a woman.

In January 2009, a senior counselor invited Wilson to participate in a new group for women "where clients could discuss gender issues associated with addiction." When some of the women complained about her participation, Phoenix House Director Sydney Hargrove allegedly told her that the counselor should have put her in a male group instead. Hargrove then initiated procedures that ultimately resulted in Wilson's removal from the treatment center. Although Wilson had excelled in the Center's career training program, had been made a "resident structure senior coordinator" and 38 men and women in her unit signed a petition calling her "a valued member of this unit" who had "earned the respect of the community," Hargrove informed Wilson that the New York district attorney would discharge her to the court if she didn't find another program to accommodate her.

Going Beyond Hate-Crime Legislation

Some LGBT groups recognize that, rather than rely on increased policing and imprisonment, they must create their own tools and strategies to address and prevent violence. In Minneapolis, understanding that discrimination and violence prevents many transgender youth from accessing social services. TYSN works with service providers to educate them about transgender issues, particularly those affecting transgender youth. By promoting awareness and education, TYSN seeks to increase safety for transgender youth in schools and social service structures, such as health care clinics, shelters and social work agencies. In addition, building awareness enables social workers and service providers to recognize and address violence and other harm when it does occur. According to Katie Burgess, this educational work builds "slow-moving but broad-reaching systems of accountability where those most affected have a voice."[2]

In New York, members of the Audre Lorde Project formed the Safe OUTside the System Collective to address street and state violence (including increased police harassment and brutality). In 2007, the collective launched the Safe Neighborhood Campaign, inviting community members to become involved in promoting personal safety. The campaign works with local businesses and other public spaces to provide safe havens from sexist, homophobic, transphobic and racist language, behavior and violence.

In the first phase of the campaign, neighborhood public spaces - such as restaurants, businesses and community groups - agree to visibly identify themselves as safe havens for those threatened with or fleeing from violence. In the next phase, the campaign incorporates an educational component. Members of the campaign train the owners and employees of the designated safe spaces, as well as other community members, on homophobia, transphobia and ways to prevent violence without relying on law enforcement.[3]

The model of the Safe Neighborhoods Campaign is one that can be replicated in other cities and by other businesses. It raises the question of what would have happened if the McDonald's in Baltimore had a safe space/no harassment policy, and if its employees had been trained to recognize and de-escalate situations before they became violent. As a Maryland-based advocate stated, shortly after the attack on Polis, "The two girls charged with the crime are in dire need of an education. Clearly they know nothing of sex and gender and have been taught that violence is acceptable." We can also ask what would have happened if the bartenders at Schooner Tavern had been trained to recognize and de-escalate situations. Would McDonald have been attacked? Would Schmitz have been stabbed?

Having tools and strategies to address, if not prevent, violence before it occurs is more effective than figuring out appropriate responses in the aftermath of trauma. Rather than advocating for greater punishment after harm has been committed, projects like TYSN and the Audre Lorde Project's Safe Neighborhoods Campaign organize communities to prevent violence before it occurs.

Endnotes

1. Interview with Katie Burgess, executive director of Trans Youth Support Network, August 24, 2011.

2. Interview with Katie Burgess, August 24, 2011.

3. Safe Neighborhood Campaign.

SEVEN

Transgender Rights Are Human Rights

Human Rights Campaign

In the following excerpted viewpoint, the Human Rights Campaign cites statistics to spotlight the alarming trend of violence and murder against transgender Americans. It then seeks to analyze the reasons for the increasing number of attacks, including intolerance, transphobia, racism, and disinterest among law enforcement officials. The result of indifference to and even promotion of prejudice against transgender individuals includes job discrimination and exclusion from healthcare and social services. Such issues are especially troubling for young trans people who have already experienced problems as they view their future lives in America and consider how they will be treated as adults. The Human Rights Campaign is America's largest civil rights organization working to achieve LGBTQ equality.

The Statistics Behind the Faces

Hate crime laws and accurate reporting of bias-motivated offenses are essential tools to understand and combat anti-transgender violence. Unfortunately, the lack of accurate and reliable data makes it impossible to know exactly how widespread anti-transgender violence really is.

Law enforcement, media outlets, and sometimes even family members often exacerbate this problem by misgendering victims, making it more difficult to gather the most accurate data. Fear of harassment from local police and social service agencies by

"A Matter of life and Death: Fatal Violence Against Transgender People in America 2016," Human Rights Campaign Foundation. Reprinted by permission.

transgender people, especially transgender women of color, also hinders accurate data collection. News media may further stigmatize victims by highlighting arrest records and using mugshots instead of personal photos when reporting their deaths.

In addition to data and reporting challenges, existing data on the size of the transgender population in the United States is limited, which complicates detailed analysis of anti-transgender violence. However, it is generally estimated that transgender women face 4.3 times the risk of becoming homicide victims than the general population of all women.

We do know this: one life lost is one too many. Since 2013, when these data were first collected:

- At least 74 transgender people were victims of fatal violence; and more than half (42) were killed by guns.

- More than 90 percent of transgender fatal violence victims were people of color (three quarters were African American).

- Nearly 9 in 10 transgender fatal violence victims were transgender women; 76 percent of victims were under the age of 35 at the time of death, with an average age of 30.

- At least 2 victims were killed by intimate partners, and at least six were killed with more than one person involved in the assault.

- Although anti-transgender violence happens across the country and in almost every state, among those reported, a plurality of victims (35 percent) were killed in the Southeast, followed by the Midwest (24 percent).

What Fuels Anti-Transgender Violence?

There are a number of factors that impact transgender people and make them particularly vulnerable to deadly violence.

First, there is the current climate of hate that normalizes and fosters discrimination and violence against the LGBTQ community. And violence, like the tragic murder of 49 LGBTQ

2016-HOM-070416

...TMENT | WASHINGTON, DC

HOMICIDE VICTIM

Ref. CCN: 16-110-051

Up to

$25,000 Reward

For information leading to the arrest
and conviction of the person(s)
responsible.
Learn more about the MPD Rewards
Program at mpdc.dc.gov/rewards

VICTIM
Gregory Dodds (AKA Deeniquia Dodds)

LOCATION
200 block of Division Avenue, NE

DATE
Wednesday, July 13, 2016

TIME
2:55 AM

CONTACT
Detective Jeffrey Weber
Detective Jeremiah Mendez

(202) 497-8616 cell
(202) 645-7288 de..
(2...) 277-...

...CRIPTION OF INCIDENT
...day, July 4, 2016 at approximately 2:55 AM, Mr...
...of Division Avenue, NE...

The trans community often feels invisible when it comes to assistance from law enforcement. Many crimes against transgender people are ignored or not reported.

people and allies at the Pulse Nightclub in Orlando, Florida, may embolden more violence.

Legislation like North Carolina's attack on the rights and dignity of the transgender community devalues the worth of transgender people. Transphobia is further compounded by racism and sexism. The rhetoric normalized during the recent presidential campaign, as well as the easy accessibility to guns, can have deadly consequences—as this report graphically shows.

Public policy and systemic issues are also major factors. Many intersect and overlap, creating more opportunities and more severe violence against transgender people, with an even greater impact on transgender women of color. The lack of, or the inability to access basic needs, like employment, transportation, stable housing and other essential services too often pushes transgender people, especially transgender women of color, into situations that leave them vulnerable to violence. It is a perfect storm, with transgender people caught in the middle. For example, the inability to access stable employment can lead transgender people to housing insecurity and lack of healthcare, which may in turn cause or further exacerbate mental and physical health problems. Economic strain may push some into underground economies like sex work, where they are further victimized, sometimes even by law enforcement.

Specifically, anti-transgender fatal violence is fueled by:

Intolerant Law Enforcement

The current justice system is one of the most significant barriers to ending anti- transgender violence in the United States. Most transgender people avoid interaction with law enforcement because they fear harassment, intimidation or incarceration—even when they themselves are the victim of a crime. Among transgender people who had interacted with police, 22 percent reported bias-based harassment from law enforcement, with transgender people of color reporting higher rates. Nearly half of all transgender people have felt uncomfortable turning to police for help.

A Cycle of Unemployment, Job Discrimination, Poverty and Survival Sex Work

In 2011, 34 percent of black and 28 percent of Latinx transgender and gender nonconforming people reported a household income of less than $10,000 per year. Transgender people are nearly four times as likely to be living in extreme poverty, with exponentially higher poverty rates for transgender people of color. Transgender people have double the national unemployment rate, with transgender people of color facing unemployment rates up to four times higher than the general population. Among the employed,

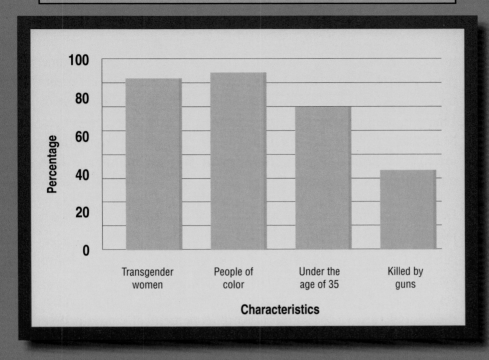

Common characteristics of transgender fatal violence victims

Source: Human Rights Campaign

90 percent of transgender people experienced harassment in the workplace, and more than 25 percent reported having lost a job because they were transgender or gender non-conforming. In the face of unemployment (and lack of benefits like health care), transgender people are often compelled to engage in underground and illegal sex work to survive. These dangerous situations put transgender people, usually transgender women of color, at a significantly higher risk of police harassment, sexual assault and fatal violence.

Exclusion from Healthcare and Social Services

An overwhelming majority of transgender and gender nonconforming people experienced discrimination by medical providers.

Too many transgender people face a medical establishment not sufficiently knowledgeable in transgender health care, and many transgender people are uninsured. As many as one in four adult, transgender women in the US is living with HIV. Forty-one percent of Black and 27 percent of Latinx transgender and gender nonconforming people have experienced homelessness at some point in their lives. Among those who tried to use homeless shelters, 29 percent of transgender people, including 40 percent of Black transgender people, have been denied access altogether. Many are evicted if staff learn they are transgender, and a plurality are forced out as a result of harassment, further enhancing their vulnerability to violence.

Disadvantaging Our Youth

Harassment, violence and discrimination faced by transgender, gender fluid and gender nonconforming youth creates real and significant barriers to education and employment. Only 43 percent of gender-expansive youth report having a family member they could turn to for support. And 78 percent of young people who described themselves as transgender or gender non-conforming reported harassment while in grades K-12. For 15 percent of these youths, the harassment was so severe that it forced them to leave school.

The Stigma of Intimate Partner Violence and Sexual Assault

For anyone, sexual violence and trauma can lead not only to injuries and health problems, but also to depression and other mental health issues that can make survivors vulnerable to revictimization. This problem is often exacerbated for transgender people, since they too often face discrimination when seeking help from shelters, law enforcement and other service providers. For transgender people who experience intimate partner violence (current or former spouse, boyfriend/ girlfriend, dating partner, ongoing sexual partner), these issues are equally acute. At least two of the 21 victims of anti-transgender homicide in 2016 were killed by intimate partners, and that number may be much higher since suspects and motives for a number of cases remain unknown.

Denying Identity

Identification documents are critical for almost every aspect of life, from daily transportation to air travel, housing to healthcare, and education to employment. For too many transgender people, obtaining accurate identity documents can often be a nightmare. Thirty-three percent of transgender people who have already transitioned report not being able to update any of their identity documents to match their affirmed gender. And of those who reported having to present documents that did not match their gender identity, almost 45 percent experienced harassment, were asked to leave or were assaulted.

EIGHT

How About Educating Everyone in School About Transgender Rights?

Brenda Alvarez

In the following viewpoint, Brenda Alvarez argues that times have changed and that schools must change with them in regard to promoting support for transgender students at all undergraduate levels. She believes that the rights that must be defended include restroom visitation based on gender identity, which has been given much attention, and also greater protection from the bullying that has targeted transgender students in recent years. Alvarez notes that students are not the only people that must be educated. She contends that parents, teachers, and administrators should receive an education about the treatment of transgender youth in their schools. Alvarez is senior writer and editor at the National Education Association.

Most students are on autopilot when it comes to the daily routine of high school. They file into first period, go from class to class, banter in the hallway, eat lunch, and take the occasional bathroom break. The transitions are processes that for the most part require little thought.

"Schools in Transition: A Guide to Support Transgender Students in K-12," by Brenda Álvarez, National Education Association, October 8, 2015. Reprinted by permission.

Educating the school population is an important step in promoting support for transgender students. Counselors and educators should be trained to understand the unique challenges faced by trans students.

For James van Kuilenburg, it's slightly different, as one of those transitions could very well be the most important decision he will make that day. What's at stake? His safety.

"I rarely use the male bathroom. It's scary," says van Kuilenburg, who came out as transgender in 2012. "There's a lot of assault—and sexual assault—in bathrooms. This isn't just in public spaces; this happens in schools, as well."

A 2013 national school climate survey conducted by GLSEN identifies the rate of verbal and physical harassment by gender identity. The findings indicate that transgender students are far more likely than other students (63 percent vs. 40 percent) to avoid bathrooms because they feel uncomfortable or unsafe.

Common forms of harassment include confrontation about using a particular restroom, homophobic and transphobic insults, people attempting to look at them while in stalls, and physical assault.

When van Kuilenburg does go, he says, "It's like a "life or death situation." He's analyzing everyone's moves. He questions: "What's the person next to me doing? If I walk in one direction, what could happen?" If he fears for his life, he won't go. This prevents him from being fully engaged in the classroom—half-listening to a lesson. It also leads to severe dehydration. But his story is not all about school bathrooms. It's about school climate and the role educators play in creating a safe and welcoming environment for all students.

A Roadmap

Many advocates say that progress has been made, but more still needs to be done. Teachers, parents, and students need to be educated, as reports from around the country continue to show parents protesting schools for allowing students to use the bathroom that matches their gender identity, or, in extreme cases, parents are bullying children.

To help the school community, the National Center for Lesbian Rights (NCLR) and Gender Spectrum, along with HRC Foundation, the American Civil Liberties Union, and the National Education Association, recently produced Schools In Transition: A Guide for Supporting Transgender Students in K-12 Schools.

The guide is a roadmap for educators and parents to provide safe and supportive environments for all transgender students, offering practical advice, field-tested tips, and narratives of real experiences from students and educators. NEA President Lily Eskelesen García has hailed this first-of-its-kind resource as a life-saver, as it comes at a time when schools are increasingly called upon to include and uphold transgender students.

"NEA is proud to be a co-author of Schools in Transition, a first-of-its kind guide to supporting transgender students in K-12 schools," said García in a joint press release from partnering

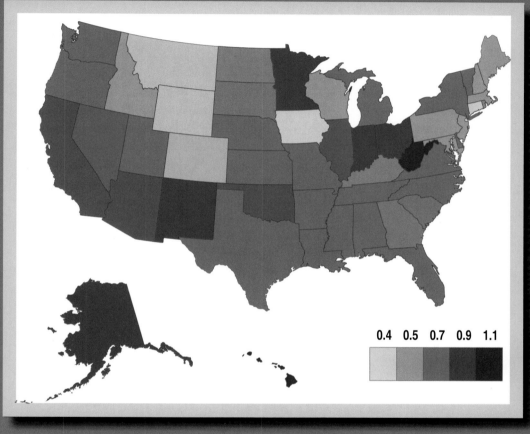

Estimated percentage of each state's population ages 13 to 17 who identify as transgender

0.4 0.5 0.7 0.9 1.1

Source: *The New York Times*

organizations. "This publication is an extremely valuable resource for the three million NEA members who work tirelessly to assure that their schools and classrooms are safe and welcoming for all students. And it will be a lifesaver for the increasing number of transgender students who are living as their authentic selves. Only when every school provides an inclusive, respectful environment can every student achieve their full potential."

The lead co-authors—Asaf Orr, transgender youth staff attorney for NCLR, and Joel Baum, senior director of professional development and family services for Gender Spectrum—say there must be more conversation and awareness around this issue so every student can thrive. Baum states that "the guide is focused on transgender students but throughout the report we talk about how important it is to create gender-inclusive conditions for every child because all kids are impacted by some of the limitations we've imposed on them related to gender." He adds, "If you wear the wrong clothes and someone makes fun of them—you become a target and there could be some real challenges."

The information in the guide is presented in an easy-to-read framework, offering information on basic concepts, including definitions for gender-expansive, transgender, and gender non-conforming. It distinguishes between gender identity and sexual orientation, which, says Baum, can be often confused as having the same meaning. Overall, schools can use the guide to help create a more welcoming environment that will increase the safety, engagement, and inclusion of every student.

Orr hopes the guide will serve as a tool to help people better understand the issue and ease some of their concerns.

Unchartered Territory

Three years ago, van Kuilenburg found himself sitting in the principal's office of his West Virginia middle school. He was 12-years old and had just shared his gender identity with the principal. He recalls the principal saying, "I just Googled what this meant and I'm wondering what you want?"

The answers were easy. He wanted to live an honest life. He wanted to feel comfortable in his own skin. He no longer wanted to cringe and suffer when someone used the wrong pronoun or the name assigned to him at birth. He wanted acceptance. He wanted acknowledgment that he had changed in a positive way. He wanted his teachers to ask him how he was doing. He wanted to be treated like a human.

Coming out, however, didn't improve his situation. He felt

alienated. He knew some students and educators were talking about him. When harassed by peers, many adults would ignore the behavior, which left him feeling unprotected.

The GLSEN survey also reveals that 62 percent of the respondents who reported harassment and assault said school staff was unresponsive. Their research emphasizes that having school support is a critical component to the success of all students. And while most reported that they had one supportive school staff member, fewer respondents could identify 11 or more.

Van Kuilenburg's "one" was a school counselor. She would approach him and ask if he needed to talk. "As soon as you have an adult on your side it validates you," he shares.

Orr explains that people are hesitant to take on this issue because this is unchartered territory. "It's not that they don't want to do it. They don't know how to respond…and they need tools to figure it out," he says. When van Kuilenburg's mom, Nicola, first spoke to the school administration, they informed her that they had no idea what to do. This resulted in a hastily prepared plan.

Around this time, Nicola crossed into Maryland to serve as UniServ director for the Maryland State Education Association, and she believes the vast majority of members are not transphobic or bigoted. She's worked with several local leaders to include gender identity in their non-discrimination policy. This was received without fanfare and an increasing number of school boards across the country are following suit. "They just need more information," she says, emphasizing that the Schools in Transition guide has been helpful.

The resource includes guidelines for meeting the needs of transgender students, addressing issues like names, pronouns, and confidentiality; restroom and locker room access; sports; and harassment or bullying. It also outlines best practices for working with unsupportive parents. An overview of the legal landscape gives administrators, educators, parents, and students more awareness of the law, as they work to create safe and supportive school environments for all.

Professional Development

While the school experience in West Virginia was unpleasant, van Kuilenburg isn't bitter about how the middle school handled his coming out. But he certainly would have felt better had the school staff been prepared with training.

Professional development is key in helping to create a more welcoming environment and helping students discover who they are in a respectful and inclusive manner. Otherwise, a transgender student will sit in silence. Author Orr states that "often times schools will say, 'This is our first transgender kid,' but we say this is the first one you know about."

The van Kuilenburgs eventually moved to Maryland so Nicola could be closer to work. But this move also provided the teen with an opportunity to start fresh. Today, van Kuilenburg attends a high school where he is "stealth," which means very few know he is transgender. There is no plan for him. He just goes to school everyday. "I walk around like any other students," he says.

He is doing well, too, and is more involved in school activities. His teachers are nice and mindful, and he finds that people are more willing to learn. If a student makes an insensitive comment, teachers will pull him aside and ask if he's okay. There are still some challenges to his school day, but for the most part, he says, "it's a lot better."

Baum understands how challenging this can be for schools and how challenging it can be initially to imagine taking this on, but schools can do this. "It's consistent with what we've done all along as educators: to meet the needs of kids…and create better learning conditions where everyone feels safe and respected."

NINE

Transgender Employees Must Be Treated with Dignity and Respect

United States Office of Personnel Management

In the following viewpoint, the United States Office of Personnel Management (OPM) sets guidelines to educate employers that their duty to treat all current and potentially future employees with respect extends to transgender men and women. It might seem strange that articulating this fact would be necessary, but the OPM assumes that many government employers could be ignorant about gender identity and equity issues and laws that regulate fair treatment. The policy serves as a tool that educates employers about how transgender employees should be addressed and treated during the hiring process and in the workplace once the individual has become part of the team. The United States Office of Personnel Management is an agency independent of the federal government that provides human resources, leadership, and support to federal agencies.

Policy and Purposes

It is the policy of the Federal Government to treat all of its employees with dignity and respect and to provide a workplace that is free from discrimination whether that discrimination is based on race, color, religion, sex (including gender identity or pregnancy), national origin, disability, political affiliation, marital status, membership in an employee organization, age, sexual orientation, or

"Guidance Regarding the Employment of Transgender Individuals in the Federal Workplace," U.S. Office of Personnel Management.

other non-merit factors. Agencies should review their anti-discrimination policies to ensure that they afford a non-discriminatory working environment to employees irrespective of their gender identity or perceived gender non-conformity.

The purpose of this memorandum is to provide guidance to address some of the common questions that agencies have raised with OPM regarding the employment of transgender individuals in the federal workplace. Because the guidance is of necessity general in nature, managers, supervisors, and transitioning employees should feel free to consult with their human resources offices and with the Office of Personnel Management to seek advice in individual circumstances.

Core Concepts

Gender identity is the individual's internal sense of being male or female. The way an individual expresses his or her gender identity is frequently called "gender expression," and may or may not conform to social stereotypes associated with a particular gender.

Transgender: Transgender individuals are people with a gender identity that is different from the sex assigned to them at birth. Someone who was assigned the male sex at birth but who identifies as female is a *transgender woman*. Likewise, a person assigned the female sex at birth but who identifies as male is a *transgender man*. Some individuals who would fit this definition of transgender do not identify themselves as such, and identify simply as men and women, consistent with their gender identity. The guidance discussed in this memorandum applies whether or not a particular individual self-identifies as transgender.

Transition: Some individuals will find it necessary to transition from living and working as one gender to another. These individuals often seek some form of medical treatment such as counseling, hormone therapy, electrolysis, and reassignment surgery. These treatments may be deemed medically necessary for many individuals, based on determinations of their medical providers. Some individuals, however, will not pursue some (or any) forms of medical treatment because of their age, medical condition, lack

Trans people are frequently discriminated against in the workforce. Some organizations, like the Transgender Economic Empowerment Initiative, place trans workers with supportive companies.

of funds, or other personal circumstances, or because they may not feel the treatment is necessary for their well-being. Managers and supervisors should be aware that not all transgender individuals will follow the same pattern, but they all are entitled to the same consideration as they undertake the transition steps deemed appropriate for them, and should all be treated with dignity and respect.

Transition While Employed

There are several issues that commonly generate questions from managers and employees who are working with a transitioning employee. In order to assist you in ensuring that transitioning employees are treated with dignity and respect, we offer the following guidance on those issues.

Confidentiality and Privacy

An employee's transition should be treated with as much sensitivity and confidentiality as any other employee's significant life experiences, such as hospitalization or family difficulties. Employees in transition often want as little publicity about their transition as possible. They may be concerned about safety and employment issues if other people or employers become aware that he or she has transitioned. Moreover, medical information received about individual employees is protected under the Privacy Act (5 U.S.C. 552a).

Employing agencies, managers, and supervisors should be sensitive to these special concerns and advise employees not to spread information concerning the employee who is in transition: gossip and rumor-spreading in the workplace about gender identity are inappropriate. Other employees may be given only general information about the employee's transition; personal information about the employee should be considered confidential and should not be released without the employee's prior agreement. Questions regarding the employee should be referred to the employee himself or herself. It should be noted, however, that questions regarding a coworker's medical process, body, and sexuality are inappropriate. If it would be helpful and appropriate, employing agencies may have a trainer or presenter meet with employees to answer general questions regarding gender identity. Issues that may arise should be discussed as soon as possible confidentially between the employee and his or her managers and supervisors.

Dress and Appearance

Agencies are encouraged to evaluate, and consider eliminating, gender-specific dress and appearance rules. Once an employee has informed management that he or she is transitioning, agency dress codes should be applied to employees transitioning to a different gender in the same way that they are applied to other employees of that gender. Dress codes should not be used to prevent a transgender employee from living full-time in the role consistent with his or her gender identity.

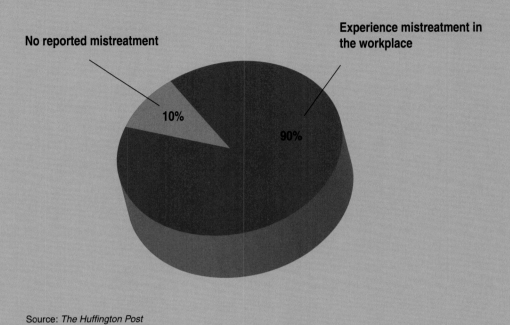

Percentage of transgender population who report experiencing mistreatment in the workplace

No reported mistreatment

Experience mistreatment in the workplace

10%

90%

Source: *The Huffington Post*

Names and Pronouns

Managers, supervisors, and coworkers should use the name and pronouns appropriate to the gender the employee is now presenting at work. Further, managers, supervisors, and coworkers should take care to use the correct name and pronouns in employee records and in communications with others regarding the employee. Continued intentional misuse of the employee's new name and pronouns, and reference to the employee's former gender by managers, supervisors, or coworkers is contrary to the goal of treating transitioning employees with dignity and respect, and creates an unwelcoming work environment. Such misuse may also breach the employee's privacy.

The Department of Labor's Occupational Safety and Health Administration (DOL/OSHA) guidelines (external link) require agencies to make access to adequate sanitary facilities as free as possible for all employees in order to avoid serious health consequences. For a transitioning employee, this means that, once he or she has begun working in the gender that reflects his or her gender identity, agencies should allow access to restrooms and (if provided to other employees) locker room facilities consistent with his or her gender identity. Transitioning employees should not be required to have undergone or to provide proof of any particular medical procedure (including gender reassignment surgery) in order to have access to facilities designated for use by a particular gender. Under no circumstances may an agency require an employee to use facilities that are unsanitary, potentially unsafe for the employee, located at an unreasonable distance from the employee's work station, or that are inconsistent with the employee's gender identity. Agencies are encouraged to provide unisex, single-user restrooms when feasible to maximize comfort and access for everyone, including individuals with disabilities and those with young children, however transgender employees should not be limited to using these facilities. Because every workplace is configured differently, agencies with questions regarding employee access to any facilities within an agency may contact OPM for further guidance.

Workplace assignments and duties:

In some workplaces, specific assignments or duties are differentiated by gender. For a transitioning employee, once he or she has begun working full-time in the gender that reflects his or her gender identity, agencies should treat the employee as that gender for purposes of all job assignments and duties. Transitioning employees should not be required to have undergone or to provide proof of any particular medical procedure (including gender reassignment surgery) in order to be eligible for gender-specific assignments or duties. Under no circumstances may an agency require an employee to accept a gender-specific assignment or duty contrary to the gender the employee otherwise works as, or limit gender-specific assignments or duties for an employee once the employee's Official Personnel Folder (OPF) has been reconstructed to reflect the new gender.

Recordkeeping

Consistent with the Privacy Act, the records in the employee's Official Personnel Folder (OPF) and other employee records (pay accounts, training records, benefits documents, and so on) should be changed to show the employee's new name and gender, once the employee has begun working full-time in the gender role consistent with the employee's gender identity and has submitted a request to update his or her OPF. See 5 U.S.C. 552a(d). Instructions for how to reconstruct an employee's OPF to account for a gender change are set forth in Chapter 4, How to Reconstruct a Personnel Folder.

Sick and Medical Leave

Employees receiving treatment as part of their transition may use sick leave under applicable regulations. Employees who are qualified under the Family Medical Leave Act may also be entitled to take medical leave for transition-related needs of their families.

Hiring Process

During the hiring process, hiring managers and supervisors should be sensitive to the possibility that applicants have transitioned. The name and gender on the application may correspond with the person's current usage; however, background or suitability checks may disclose a previous name that indicates a gender different from the one the applicant is currently presenting. In such cases, hiring managers should respectfully ask whether the applicant was previously known by a different name, and confirm with the applicant the name and gender that should be used throughout the hiring process.

Insurance Benefits

Employees in transition who already have Federal insurance benefits must be allowed to continue their participation, and new employees must be allowed to elect participation, based on their updated names and genders. If the employees in transition are validly married at the time of the transition, the transition does not affect the validity of that marriage, and spousal coverage should be extended or continued even though the employee in transition has a new name and gender. Further information about insurance coverage issues can be found on the web at OPM's Insure website, or by contacting the relevant OPM insurance program office.

TEN

Equal Opportunity in the Military Must Include Transgender Servicepeople

Ash Carter

> In the following viewpoint, transcribed from a press briefing, former Secretary of Defense Ash Carter details a series of changes instituted in 2016 that sought to make the United States military more inclusive. The right of LGBTQ individuals to serve in the US military has been a significant topic of discussion in recent years. Ash's announcement explained that, for the US military to remain as strong as possible, all Americans regardless of gender identity must receive equal access to acceptance into the various branches of the military, as well as equal treatment once that individual is in the service. Carter served as US Secretary of Defense during the Obama administration.

I am here today to announce some changes in the Defense Department's policies regarding transgender service members. And before I announce what changes we're making, I want to explain why.

"Department of Defense Press Briefing by Secretary Carter on Transgender Service Policies in the Pentagon Briefing Room," by Ash Carter, U.S. Department of Defense, June 30, 2016.

There are three main reasons, having to do with their future force, our current force and matters of principle. The first and fundamental reason is that the Defense Department and the military need to avail ourselves of all talent possible in order to remain what we are now, the finest fighting force the world has ever known.

Our mission is to defend this country and we don't want barriers unrelated to a person's qualification to serve preventing us from recruiting or retaining the soldier, sailor, airman or Marine who can best accomplish the mission.

We have to have access to 100 percent of America's population for our all-volunteer force to be able to recruit from among them the most highly qualified and to retain them.

Now, while there isn't definitive data on the number of transgender service members, RAND looked at the existing studies out there, and their best estimate was that about 2,500 people out of approximately 1.3 million active-duty service members, and about 1,500 out of 825,000 reserve service members are transgender, with the upper end of their range of estimates of around 7,000 in the active component and 4,000 in the reserves.

Although relatively few in number, we're talking about talented and trained Americans who are serving their country with honor and distinction. We invest hundreds of thousands of dollars to train and develop each individual, and we want to take the opportunity to retain people whose talent we've invested in and who have proven themselves.

And this brings me to the second reason, which is that the reality is that we have transgender service members serving in uniform today. And I have a responsibility to them and to their commanders to provide them both with clearer and more consistent guidance than is provided by current policies.

We owe commanders better guidance on how to handle questions such as deployment, medical treatment and other matters. And this is particularly true for small unit leaders, like our senior enlisted and junior officers. Also, right now, most of our transgender service members must go outside the military

In 2015, the US Department of Defense recognized the need to be inclusive toward transgender service members by officially changing discriminatory and unsupportive policies.

medical system in order to obtain medical care is judged by doctors to be necessary, and they have to pay for it out of their own pockets. This is inconsistent with our promise to all our troops that we will take care of them and pay for necessary medical treat.

I, and the Defense Department's other senior leaders who have been studying this issue the past year, have met with some of these transgender service members. They've deployed all over the world, serving on aircraft, submarines, forward operating bases and right here in the Pentagon. And while I learned that in most cases, their peers and local commanders have recognized the value of retaining such high-quality people, I also learned the lack of clear

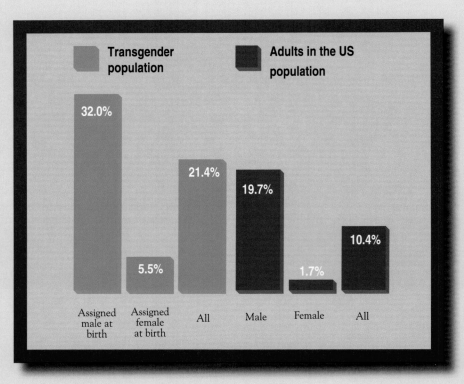

Percentage of population that has served in the military, transgender population compared to total adults in the US population

Transgender population   **Adults in the US population**

- 32.0% — Assigned male at birth
- 5.5% — Assigned female at birth
- 21.4% — All
- 19.7% — Male
- 1.7% — Female
- 10.4% — All

Source: Williams Institute

guidelines for how to handle this issue puts the commanders and the service members in a difficult and unfair position.

One service member I met with described how some people had urged him to leave the military, because of the challenges he was facing with our policies, and he said he just wouldn't quit. He was too committed to the mission, and this is where he wanted to be. These are the kind of people we want serving in our military.

The third and final reason for the change, also important, is a matter of principle. Americans who want to serve and can meet our standards should be afforded the opportunity to compete to do so. After all, our all-volunteer force is built upon having the most qualified Americans, and the profession of arms is based on honor and trust.

Army Chief-of-Staff General Milley recently reminded us of this when he said, and I quote him, "The United States Army is open to all Americans who meet the standard, regardless of who they are. Embedded within our Constitution is that very principle, that all Americans are free and equal. And we, as an Army, are sworn to protect and defend that very principle. And we are sworn to even die for that principle. So, if we in uniform are willing to die for that principle, then we in uniform should be willing to live by that principle." That's General Milley.

In view of these three reasons to change our policy, last July I directed the commencement of a study to identify the practical issues related to transgender Americans serving openly, and to develop an implementation plan that addresses those issues consistent with military readiness, because our mission -- which is defending the country -- has to come first.

[...]

Now, as a result of this year-long study, I'm announcing today that we're ending the ban on transgender Americans in the United States military.

Effective immediately, transgender Americans may serve openly and they can no longer be discharged or otherwise separated from the military just for being transgender.

Additionally, I have directed that the gender identity of an otherwise qualified individual will not bar them from military service or from any accession program.

In taking the steps, we are eliminating policies that can result in transgender members being treated differently from their peers based solely upon their gender identity, rather than upon their ability to serve and we are confirming that going forward we will apply the same general principles, standards and procedures to transgender service members as we do to all service members.

What I heard from the transgender service members I met with overwhelmingly was that they don't want special treatment. They want to be held to the same standards and be treated like everybody else.

As I directed, the study identified practical issues that arise with respect to transgender service, and it developed an implementation plan to address those issues.

[...]

I want to close by emphasizing that deliberate and thoughtful implementation will be key. I, and the senior leaders of the department will therefore be ensuring all issues identified in this study are addressed in implementation.

I'm confident they can and will be addressed in implementation. That's why we are taking the step-by-step approach I've described. And I'm 100 percent confident in the ability of our military leaders and all men and women in uniform to implement these changes in a manner that both protects the readiness of the force and also upholds values cherished by the military -- honor, trust and judging every individual on their merits.

I'm also confident that we have reason to be proud today of what this will mean for our military, because it is the right thing to do, and it's another step in ensuring that we continue to recruit and retain the most qualified people.

And good people are the key to the best military in the world. Our military and the nation it defends will be stronger.

ELEVEN

Voter ID Laws Are Unfair to Trans Voters

German Lopez

In the following viewpoint, German Lopez contends that voting has become a struggle for the transgender population due to stricter voter identification laws. While these laws don't specifically target trans people, they can end up affecting them the most. This is due to the simple fact that trans people's official forms of identification often don't match up with their names, genders, and physical appearances because the changing of such information is prohibited in many states. Lopez suggests that ending such restrictions would save states from causing confusion. Most importantly, it would provide all citizens with access to the ballot box. Lopez is Senior Reporter at Vox Media and writes extensively on LGBTQ issues.

O ver the past few years, more and more states have passed strict voter ID laws. Much of the attention around these laws has gone to how they tend to target people of color and make it much harder for them to vote. And the evidence certainly suggests these laws do target, sometimes intentionally so, and harm voters of color.

But there's another marginalized segment of the population that can be greatly hurt by strict voter ID laws: transgender people.

"Trans people are not specifically targeted by any voter ID laws," Arli Christian, state policy counsel for the National Center

"States Are Making It A Lot Harder for Transgender People to Vote," by German Lopez, Vox Media, Inc., October 25, 2016. Reprinted by permission.

Trans people are impeded from voting when states have strict voter identification laws. Hurdles such as these are covert forms of discrimination faced by transgender individuals.

for Transgender Equality (NCTE), told me. "However, voter ID laws have a disproportionate effect on transgender communities."

Once you think about it, these hurdles are pretty obvious. For example, a trans person's legal name, photo, or gender marker just may not be updated on a legal ID, because state law makes it difficult or impossible to alter that kind of information. So when trans people show up at the polling booth, they may have their identities questioned and denied because their physical appearance doesn't match what their ID says. And that could hinder trans people's ability to vote, or stop them from voting altogether.

Strict Voter ID Laws Make it Especially Harder for Trans People to Vote

This situation is enabled by state laws that are very strict in what kind of ID is required to vote — Texas, for example, allows a driver's license or other government-issued ID, but not a student ID or bank statement. States can also make it difficult to update the name, photo, or gender marker on government-issued IDs.

According to NCTE, five states have strict voter ID laws *and* make it very difficult or even impossible for trans people to change the gender markers on their IDs: Alabama, Georgia, Kansas, Mississippi, and Tennessee.

"Transgender voters in those states are left with few options," Christian said. "They may try to meet the burdensome requirements for updating the gender marker on their ID if they are able. They may brave it and head to the polls with an ID that does not match who they are, opening themselves up to potential harassment and unnecessary scrutiny and suspicion from poll workers. Or they may decide not to vote at all."

The five states are the worst offenders, but other states have a variety of hurdles that can make it difficult to vote. In general, updating ID documents is "a fairly complicated process," Christian explained. Whether it's changing a legal name, getting a new photo, or altering other information, many people simply don't have the time or resources — particularly transportation — that may be required to get to, say, a court or DMV.

But perhaps the biggest hurdle is many states' requirements for changing a gender marker. States can require, for instance, proof of surgery or a doctor's signature to get a gender marker changed on birth certificates or government-issued IDs. Some, like Tennessee, don't let you change certain documents at all.

The result is that trans people often face problems — not just in polling booths, but broadly — due to outdated IDs. According to the 2011 National Trans Discrimination Survey, 40 percent of trans people reported harassment or discrimination when presenting an ID that doesn't match who they are. And only one-fifth of those who transitioned were able to change all of their documentation and records.

It doesn't have to be this way, especially to exercise a citizen's most basic right.

Transitioning Is an Individual, Private Process. States' ID Laws Breach that Privacy.

The main problem with laws around IDs and gender transitioning is they assume that transitioning is a uniform process for all trans people. They are essentially relics of the 1970s, when surgery in particular was deemed the one standard for proving someone's gender identity — even though not all trans people want or can get the surgeries that states deem necessary, even if they alter other aspects of their physical appearance to match their gender identity.

"Gender transition is an individually unique process," Christian said. "Transitioning may include things like changing a legal name or just changing a name used in social settings, changing gender pronouns, changing someone's dress and gender expression; [it] may include hormone therapy, may include surgery or other medical intervention, may include working with a therapist to explore gender identity. These are all different aspects of gender transition that an individual may go through. And there's no one right, prescribed way to transition."

The 2011 National Trans Discrimination Survey bears this out: It found that about 61 percent of trans and gender nonconforming

States with strict photo identification voting laws and the number and percentage of transgender people without updated identification

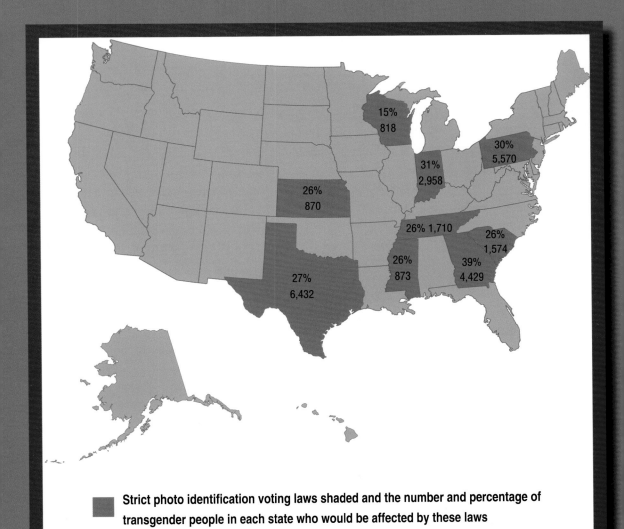

Strict photo identification voting laws shaded and the number and percentage of transgender people in each state who would be affected by these laws

Source: Williams Institute

respondents reported having medically transitioned, and 33 percent said they had surgically transitioned. And about 14 percent of trans women and 72 percent of trans men said they don't ever want full genital construction surgery. That's a lot of trans people, particularly trans men, who would not meet requirements for changing their IDs in some states.

There are many reasons why this is the case. Some trans people may not be able to afford all the surgeries required. Some may have medical conditions that inhibit some or all of these surgeries. And some may simply not want to get the procedures done — they may consider the surgeries too invasive, or they may think the surgeries shouldn't be and aren't necessary to identify and express as a certain gender.

So some trans people may look like and present as the gender they identify as but not get some of the surgeries required to change a state ID. And that could lead to problems at the polls.

There's another side to this: privacy concerns. Some trans people may not want to tell everyone that they are trans — perhaps out of fear of discrimination or stigmatization, including from government officials.

Yet states' ID requirements can effectively force trans people to disclose their medical information and transition history to vote. "Medical information is private, is between an individual and their doctor, and should not be requested by the state in order to get an ID that reflects who you are," Christian said.

States Can Ease ID Hurdles that Trans People Face and Potentially Save Time and Money

To make it easier for trans people to vote, states could repeal strict voter ID laws in the first place. But short of that, states could make it easier to change information on an ID.

NCTE, for one, recommends that states allow a simple one-page form that lets someone indicate the relevant information for an ID, including gender markers. And, Christian said, states should stop requiring that a health care provider sign off on these kinds of forms.

Reforms in this area could simplify or eliminate a process that currently requires several parts of government — courts and police in particular — to spend time and resources policing someone's gender by imposing hurdles to legally transitioning. And it makes voting more difficult, but it can also unnecessarily complicate anything from a trip to the bathroom to a routine traffic stop to renewing a driver's license.

"When we don't allow people to update their ID to reflect who they are, we are doing a disservice to law enforcement, to poll officials, to society," Christian argued, "because we're making it more complicated and confusing."

For now, trans people can access some resources to try to have an easier time voting at NCTE's website. And if trans voters run into problems, NCTE recommends trying to find help first at a local polling place (where volunteers may help), calling the national Election Protection hotline (1-866-OUR-VOTE) for aid, and, as a last resort, obtaining a provisional ballot to vote.

But maybe voting just shouldn't be this hard for anyone in the first place.

TWELVE

The Justice System Is Failing Transgender Individuals

Samantha Pegg

> In the following viewpoint, Samantha Pegg asserts that the treatment of transgender prisoners should be closely examined and reformed. Pegg cites the death of transgender woman Vikki Thompson, who was placed in a men's prison in the United Kingdom and died under mysterious circumstances a month after arriving. The author offers that the cases of Thompson and others should motivate criminal justice systems to study and revise their policies as they affect their transgender communities so that such tragedies would be far less likely to occur. Pegg is Senior Lecturer in Criminal Law at Nottingham Trent University in England.

The death of transgender woman Vikki Thompson, 21, who was serving her sentence at the all-male Armley Prison in Leeds has drawn attention once again to the treatment of transgender persons by the criminal justice system.

Since the UK Gender Recognition Act 2004 came into force, transgender people have been able to have their acquired gender recognised by going through a detailed legal process which, if satisfied, allows a new birth certificate to be issued. For legal purposes

"Legal Certificate or Not, Trans People Deserve Better From The Prison System," by Samantha Pegg, The Conversation, November 21, 2015. https://theconversation.com/legal-certificate-or-not-trans-people-deserve-better-from-the-prison-system-51069. Licensed Under CC BY ND 4.0 International.

Transgender prisoners face harassment and dangerous conditions when they are placed among the gender they no longer identify with.

the applicant is then recognised in their new gender. While this was a valuable step toward recognising gender autonomy it seems to have created a hierarchy for trans people, one that permeates our legal and criminal justice system.

As Thompson had no "gender recognition certificate" she was placed in prison estate that reflected her birth gender. This is in line with the National Offender Management Service guidance that requires prisoners to be placed according to their gender as recognised by the law. There are clearly problems in terms of prison estate – housing those transitioning from male to female in female prisons have in some cases been deemed to raise issues of safety for other inmates.

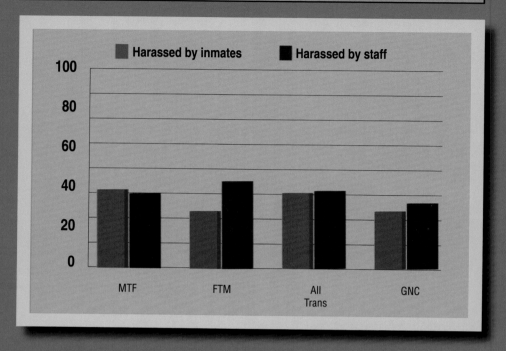

Percentage of transgender and gender nonconforming inmates who experience harassment in jail or prison

Harassed by inmates Harassed by staff

MTF   FTM   All Trans   GNC

Source: National Center for Transgender Equality/National Gay and Lesbian Task Force

There is some discretion in this policy, where transgender people are "sufficiently advanced in the gender reassignment process" they may be placed "in the estate of their acquired gender". This was the case for Tara Hudson, the transgender woman initially held in an all-male prison who complained of sexual harassment. Hudson was moved to a female facility after significant public attention prompted the Prison Service to recognise that, as she had lived as a woman all her adult life and had undergone gender reconstruction surgery, she was – in all but law – female.

It is this legal recognition of gender that is the sticking point. The death of Thompson will undoubtedly prompt a rethink of the current rules governing the placement of prisoners – and indeed an investigation is underway. But until there is clearer guidance and rights for trans people, there may be more tragic stories like Thompson's.

Self-identification

The convictions of Gayle Newland and Justine McNally for sexual offences that involved deceiving others about their gender, show how complicated it can be if someone self-identifies as a trans person but is not legally transitioned.

Both were recognised as suffering from gender confusion and, although both had sought psychiatric help for issues including anxiety and self-harm, neither was undergoing medical or legal transition. The fact they had then misrepresented their gender was considered to be something which had prevented their victims making a fully informed decision about consent. That these young women had lied was central to the convictions here – that the defendants may have self-identified as male at the time of the offences was given little credence.

The law here seems to be fixated on binary gender roles with little tolerance for gender variance. However whether their actions would have been adjudged criminal if Newland and McNally had legally transitioned is also still unclear. It is certainly relevant to prosecutions for sexual offences and the Crown Prosecution Service has advised that, when an offence involves a transgender suspect, "prosecutors will need to know the suspect's position in relation to the Gender Recognition Act 2004 (GRA)".

While it is unsurprising that criminal law has struggled to deal sensitively with gender confusion, the rules governing prison placements are slightly clearer – although they still focus on whether the prisoner has undergone legal recognition.

Holding "Proof"

If we consider possession of a gender recognition certificate definitive proof of gender we need to open up access to those services that allow people to address this, specifically gender identity clinics. There are a limited number of these clinics and UKTrans, an organisation working to campaign and provide advice for trans and non-binary people, [report](http://uktrans.info/waitingtimes the waiting time for an appointment stands (as of September 2015) at anything from six weeks to 3.5 years, with most clinics reporting a waiting time of more than a year. It is clear that those suffering gender confusion will currently have a long wait to access services.

What of those who haven't accessed these services, should we treat them in their acquired gender regardless of their position vis-a-vis the law? This will be a question for the transgender equality inquiry by the women and equalities select committee that recently concluded. Tasked with looking at our treatment of trans people, the inquiry will be considering issues affecting trans people in the criminal justice system and access to services.

Addressing these issues is becoming increasingly important. In a society that supports the rights of individuals to live unmolested in their chosen gender role we need to think very carefully about how to treat those who are not legally recognised in their acquired gender.

What You Should Know About Transgender Rights

Facts About Transgender People

- The number of transgender people in the United States is unknown. One estimate in 2015 stated the approximate number as seven hundred thousand, or 0.3 percent of all Americans. But the Williams Institute estimated the number as 1.4 million.

- One survey of transgender Americans revealed that 41 percent had attempted suicide at one point, due greatly to bullying, sexual assault, or job loss.

- Poverty is a major issue among trans people, who are four times more likely to have an annual household income of $10,000 or less.

- About 20 percent of all transgender Americans have reported being homeless at one point. Nearly one quarter of those claimed to have been sexually assaulted during that period.

- A bit more than one in ten among the transgender population in the United States has claimed to have been evicted from their homes due to bias.

- The National Center for Transgender Equality and the National Gay and Lesbian Task Force report that nearly one in five transgender people have been refused health care due to their gender status.

- A survey taken by Injustice at Every Turn revealed that one in four American transgender individuals have lost their jobs because they did not conform to gender norms.

- The Williams Institute in 2015 estimated that the US military employed fifteen thousand transgender servicepeople.

- About 16 percent of all Americans claim to know of at least one transgender person.

- According to the National Coalition of Anti-Violence Programs, 55 percent of all reported LGBT homicide victims were transgender women, and 50 percent were transgender women of color.

- More than three-fourths of all transgender/gender non-conforming students in grades K–12 experienced harassment, according to the National Transgender Discrimination Survey.

- Physical assault was reported by 35 percent of all transgender/gender non-conforming students in grades K–12; 12 percent experienced sexual violence.

- Nineteen states, including the District of Columbia, have antidiscrimination laws and ordinances providing transgender people access to public facilities that respond to their gender identity. There has been no evidence that such laws have led to violence.

- The state of Maine has maintained gender identity protections in its state civil rights law for more than a decade. No incidents have ever been reported, according to its Human Rights Commission.

- A large majority of mainstream medical, psychiatric, and psychological communities agree that being transgender is not a mental illness, but rather a valid state in which one's gender does not match what was assigned at birth.

- The American College of Pediatrics, which does not support allowing transgender children to transition at an early age, should not be confused with the American Academy of Pediatrics, which takes the opposite view. The former has only a few hundred members while the latter boasts about sixty-four thousand.

- Caitlyn Jenner is perhaps the most famous transgender person. She transitioned from Bruce Jenner, who gained fame as an Olympic gold medalist in the decathlon.

- The first transgender surgery in the United States was performed in 1967, a year after the first gender identity clinic opened at Johns Hopkins University.

- There is no average cost to gender reassignment surgery. Surgeries can run anywhere from $5,000 to $100,000.

- Though harassment at work for trans people remains common, more than three-quarters have reported that they feel more comfortable in the workplace after undergoing the transition.

- More than half of all transgender students have reported that they have been verbally abused at school, according to the Human Rights Campaign.

- One 2013 survey revealed that about one half of all transgender men and women suffer from depression. That far surpasses the percentage of the overall population.

- More than four-fifths of all transgender students report that they do not feel safe on school grounds.

- According to the American Academy of Pediatrics, transgender children feeling uncomfortable entering a bathroom often refrain from going at all, which furthers the risk of stress and urinary tract infections.

- The Centers for Disease Control and Prevention does not plan on adding a question about gender identity to its adolescent health survey until after 2019. That means it could be several or even many years before accurate data is available about transgender youths.

- About 1.5 percent of youths identify as transgender, according to polls taken in Massachusetts and Wisconsin.

- A 2016 study of 250 in the LBGT community that was published in the *American Journal of Public Health* stated that those who suffered harassment as teens went on to experience lasting mental health damage, including post-traumatic stress disorder (PTSD).

- An alarming three-fifths of transgender college students who were denied the use of bathrooms or campus housing that correspond to their gender identities have attempted suicide at least once, according to a study published in *The Journal of Homosexuality*.

- Studies have shown that transgender youth who felt supported in their decisions to transition had normal levels of depression and only slightly raised levels of anxiety.

- Gender identity and sexual orientation are unrelated. The former is what we see ourselves as being. The other is what gender and sex to which we are physically and romantically attracted.

- School officials cannot legally disclose a student's LGBT status without his or her permission.

- San Francisco was the first city to cover the cost of gender reassignment surgery.

- Conversion therapy targeting the LGBT community has not only proven unsuccessful, but psychologically harmful as well, according to the Human Rights Campaign.

- Ten states have enacted laws to prevent licensed mental health providers from offering conversion therapy to minors and another twenty states have introduced similar legislation.

- Many transgender prisoners are placed in solitary confinement for months or even years simply because of their gender identity.

- Screening techniques at airports have resulted in particular concerns of transgender people, who can be outed against their will or face bias and harassment. The procedures can prove particularly traumatic for transgender youth.

• Trans people often face barriers when seeking to foster or adopt children, according to the National Center for Transgender Equality.

• A Transgender Day of Remembrance has been declared for November 20. It is a day of mourning for transgender people who have been murdered for their gender identities.

• High unemployment and poverty have led one in eight transgender individuals to become involved in underground economic work, such as those involved with sex and drugs, in order to survive.

• Despite the passage of the Affordable Care Act, which has since come under attack, most public and private insurance plans still include discriminatory exclusions for transgender-related care.

What You Should Do About Transgender Rights

It is important to be aware of expert conclusions that have been made in recent years regarding transgender people. A significant majority of specialists in the field believe that those who have undergone gender reassignment surgery or who identify with a gender not assigned at birth have made healthy life decisions. They are who they know they are.

But that is not the most critical issue for those associated with trans people, whether they be friends, fellow students, co-workers, or family members. The fact is that everyone has feelings and transgender people are more vulnerable emotionally than others, having made a brave decision that places them in a tiny minority among the world population.

In the hearts and minds of millions, that makes them different. And to the bigoted and intolerant, being different makes trans people an easy target of jokes and ridicule, even physical abuse. It is the duty of everyone to not only take steps to prevent such occurrences but also to make people in the transgender community feel comfortable in social situations and in all aspects of their lives through support and inclusion.

Students who are transgender or struggling with gender identity are particularly vulnerable because teenagers have yet to reach a maturity level that allows them to fully comprehend such changes in their lives or emotionally cope with becoming the target of harassment. And school-age individuals might be less likely to accept transgender peers and more likely to bully them.

Schools are sometimes breeding grounds for behavior that can prove devastating to transgender students. That means the positive forces in their lives inside and outside school must far outweigh the negative ones. Many avenues for promoting a healthy environment can be explored.

Among them is to make sure the school they attend has a written policy against discrimination based on gender identity or expression. Another is to ensure that the school codes have a strong antiharassment and antibullying policy that includes gender identity and expression. The students, faculty, and administration should be aware of such policies and be vigilant about enforcing them. Also, any school groups or clubs that advocate for gay students should back their transgender peers as well.

There are more personal, one-on-one approaches to make life more comfortable and inclusive for transgender students. One is to simply befriend the individual and let him or her know that you care. Another is to speak out against antitransgender jokes inside and outside school grounds, even when there are no transgender people around. Those that realize that it is not acceptable to joke about gender identity are far less likely to abuse or harass a trans peer.

Such support is critical for transgender people who might be struggling due to rejection from friends and family members or simply due to discrimination against them. Do not be afraid to express feelings of support. It is also important to confront those who are meting out physical or emotional abuse or have unfriended a transgender person due to his or her transition. Every piece of evidence about those that have undergone gender reassignment surgery proves that the person needs a supportive friend more than ever. Friends should even find a place to stay for a trans teen who has been unfairly kicked out of their home.

Transgender people and their friends should understand that they are not alone in their struggles. Organizations that support the LGBTQ community abound. They should be contacted not only to register complaints about discrimination but also for advice on how to combat emotional or physical abuse. One can also create programs along with local or state governments or LGBTQ community centers that can assist transgender individuals in the realms of housing, education, and job training. Such organizations can ensure that local communities are strongly transgender-inclusive.

The more that young people understand about the obstacles facing the transgender community, the greater their ability to help. Gaining knowledge about all aspects of their potential struggles will always prove beneficial. Aspects of their daily lives such as state laws regarding public accommodations, health and social service systems, and legal rights must be fully grasped for one to even begin to understand the size of the hill that transgender people must climb to secure the opportunities to succeed that should be afforded all citizens.

It is not enough to not participate in negative treatment of transgender people one might know. One cannot simply look the other way. If everyone embraced an empathetic view based on the wise adage about treating people the way they would like to be treated, the transgender population would feel far more comfortable and less fearful about their transitions. We must all fight for trans rights. Only when everyone in our society is treated with the same measure of respect and dignity can Americans live up to the creed of the nation that all people are created equal.

The editors have compiled the following list of organizations concerned with the issues debated in this book. The descriptions are derived from materials provided by the organizations. All have publications or information available for interested readers. The list was compiled on the date of publication of the present volume; the information provided here may change. Be aware that many organizations take several weeks or longer to respond to inquiries, so allow as much time as possible.

Gay & Lesbian Alliance Against Defamation (GLAAD)
5455 Wilshire Blvd.
No. 1500
Los Angeles, CA 90036
(323) 933-2240
website: https://www.glaad.org

GLAAD works toward greater societal acceptance of transgender people and others in the LGBT community.

Gay, Lesbian, and Straight Education Network (GLSEN)
110 William Street.
30th Floor
New York, NY 10038
(212) 727-0135
email: info@glsen.org
website: https://www.glsen.org

The mission of GLSEN is to create safe and affirming schools for all, regardless of sexual orientation, gender identity, or gender expression.

Human Rights Campaign
1540 Rhode Island Avenue NW
Washington, DC 20036-3278
(202) 628-4160

email: feedback@hrc.org
website: www.hrc.org

HRC is the largest civil rights organization for the LGBT community, counting among them 1.5 million members.

National Center for Transgender Equality

1400 16th Street NW
Suite 510
Washington, DC 20036
(202) 642-4542
email: ncte@transequality.org
website: www.transequality.org

The NCTE is the leading advocacy group for transgender people. It has worked to help gain positive changes for the transgender community.

National LBGTQ Task Force

1325 Massachusetts Avenue NW
Suite 600
Washington, DC 20005
(202) 393-5177
website: www.thetaskforce.org/contact.html

The Task Force works to remove barriers from the lives of LGBTQ people in the areas of housing, employment, healthcare, and basic human rights.

National Transgender Advocacy Coalition

3623 Old Charleston Highway
PO Box 22088
Charleston. SC 29413-2088
(843) 883-0343
website: http://affa-sc.org/contact

This lobbying organization is part of the Alliance for Full Acceptance, a social justice organization that seeks to achieve equality and acceptance for the LGBT community.

Parents, Families, and Friends of Lesbians & Gays
1828 L Street NW
Suite 660
Washington, DC 20036
(202) 467-8180
email: info@pflag..org
website: www.pflag.org

PFLAG has more than four hundred chapters that offer confidential peer support, education, and advocacy in communities for LGBT people.

Transgender Foundation of America
604 Pacific
Houston, TX 77006
(713) 520-8586
website: www.tfahouston.com

The Transgender Foundation of America seeks to improve the lives of transgender people through various means, such as homeless services, counseling, and group therapy.

Trans Youth Equality Foundation (TYEF)
PO Box 7441
Portland, ME 04112-7441
website: www.transyouthequality.org/our-mission/

The TYEF is a national nonprofit that advocates for transgender, gender nonconforming, and intersex youth ages 2–18.

BIBLIOGRAPHY

Books

Arin Andrews, *Some Assembly Required: The Not-So-Secret Life of a Transgender Teen.* New York, N.Y.: Simon & Schuster, 2015.
This memoir describes the challenges of the author's transition.

Kathleen Archambeau, *Pride & Joy: LGBTQ Artists, Icons, and Everyday Heroes.* Coral Gables, FL: Mango Publishing Group, 2017.
This book encourages LGBTQ citizens of the world to live open, happy, fulfilling, strong, and successful lives.

Marty Gitlin, *Chaz Bono (Transgender Pioneers).* New York, N.Y.: Rosen Publishing, 2016.
This biography describes the emotional turmoil of the son of superstar singer and actress Cher. Bono's transition opened the eyes of many Americans to trans issues.

Walt Heyer, *A Transgender's Faith.* CreateSpace Independent Publishing Platform, 2015.
This book tells the true story of man plagued since childhood with the feelings that he should have been a girl. His torment intensifies as he ages, marries, and starts a family.

Katie Rain Hill, *Rethinking Normal: A Memoir in Transition.* New York, N.Y.: Simon & Schuster, 2015.
This memoir of a transgender woman raised as a boy describes her strained family relationships and struggles as she underwent her transition.

Jazz Jennings, *Being Jazz, My Life as a (Transgender) Teen.* New York, N.Y.: Crown Books for Young Readers, 2016.
YouTube personality Jazz Jennings shares her school experiences, including her battles to play on the girls' soccer team and use the girls' bathroom. This book seeks to educate others about the obstacles faced by transgender students.

Susan Kuklin. *Beyond Magenta: Transgender Teens Speak Out.* Somerville, MA: Candlewick Press, 2015.
Six transgender teens describe their trials and tribulations. Included is their coming out, as well as their relationships with family and friends.

Amy Ellis Nutt, *Becoming Nicole: The Transformation of an American Family*. New York, N.Y.: Random, House, 2015.
This account of the transformation of a conservative American family describes how family members worked to accept the transition of one of their own.

RyLan Jay Testa, *The Gender Quest Workbook: A Guide for Teens and Young Adults Exploring Gender Identity*. Oakland, CA: Instant Help, 2015.
This guide is designed for teens interested in exploring gender through steps that develop identity and comfort with oneself.

Periodicals and Internet Sources

Michael J. Broyde, "Transgender bathroom issue: a solution?" *CNN*, October 26, 2016.
http://www.cnn.com/2016/10/28/opinions/the-bathroom-issue-were-not-talking-about/index.html

Niraj Chokshi. "One in every 137 teenagers would identify as transgender, report says," *New York Times*, February 23, 2017.
https://www.nytimes.com/2017/02/23/us/transgender-teenagers-how-many.html

Wynne Davis and Von Diaz, "Transgender boy finds his 'bros,' and himself, at camp," *NPR.org*, March 3, 2017.
http://www.npr.org/2017/03/03/518206326/transgender-boy-finds-his-bros-and-himself-at-camp

Rebecca Hersher, "Some teachers, principals and students condemn Trump transgender policy," *NPR.org*, February 23, 2017.
http://www.npr.org/sections/thetwo-way/2017/02/23/516878336/some-teachers-principals-and-students-condemn-trump-transgender-policy

Jenny Kleeman, "Transgender children: 'This is who he is – I have to respect that,'" *The Guardian*, September 12, 2015.
https://www.theguardian.com/society/2015/sep/12/transgender-children-have-to-respect-who-he-is

Cynthia Miller-Idriss, "My daughter's favorite teacher is transgender: Here's why that matter," *Huffington Post*, June 21, 2017.

http://www.huffingtonpost.com/entry/my-daughters-fa-vorite-teacher-is-transgender-heres_us_594aa2a1e4b-062254f3a5ac7?utm_hp_ref=transgender

Diana Pearl and Elizabeth Leonard, "Why Caitlyn Jenner decided to undergo sex reassignment surgery," *People*, April 11, 2017. http://people.com/books/caitlyn-jenner-confirms-she-under-went-gender-reassignment-surgery-in-new-memoir/

Francine Russo, "Is there something unique about the transgender brain?" *Scientific American*, January 1, 2016. https://www.scientificamerican.com/article/is-there-something-unique-about-the-transgender-brain/

Kirsten Salyer, "Transgender teen: Bathroom equality is a civil rights issue," *Time Magazine*, May 16, 2016. http://time.com/4330120/transgender-bathroom-equality/

Nina Shapiro, "Transgender kids: a family quest, a medical quan-dary," *Seattle Times*, October 7, 2016. http://www.seattletimes.com/seattle-news/health/transgender-kids-a-family-quest-a-medical-quandary/

Thomas Wheatley. "Transgender bathroom users will not endan-ger women, but twisted social norms might," *Washington Post*, January 27, 2017. https://www.washingtonpost.com/blogs/all-opinions-are-local/wp/2017/01/27/transgender-bathroom-users-will-not-endanger-women-but-twisted-social-norms-might/?utm_ter-m=.388249e4c336

Websites

Human Rights Campaign
www.hrc.org/

The site for an organization that fights for equality features news articles about transgender rights, as well as the rights of all in the LGBT community. The Human Rights Campaign seeks donations to help the cause of transgender people and others.

Gay/Straight Alliance Network

https://gsanetwork.org/what-we-do/transforming-schools

An organization that seeks to make schools a safe and uplifting environment for transgender students and others boasts a website that trumpets news and events about LGBT issues. It teaches what people can do to help.

Gender Diversity

www.genderdiversity.org/

This website works to increase the awareness and understanding of gender diversity in children, teens, and adults by promoting family support. It seeks to build community, increase awareness, and improve the lives of people of all gender identities and expressions.

INDEX

Equality Maryland, 45

F
Family Medical Leave Act, 71
Family Research Council, 33
federal government, 6, 22, 31,
   65, 68, 72

G
Gallo, William, 8
Garcia, Lily Eskelesen, 60
gender identity, 45–46, 48,
   57, 58–60, 62, 65–66, 68,
   70–71, 73, 77, 82, 89
gender identity disorder, 30,
   34,
Gender Recognition Act of
   2004 (GRA), 86, 89
Gender Spectrum, 60, 62
GLSEN, 59, 63
Gorman, Anna, 29
government overreach, 18–19

H
harassment, 44, 49–51, 54–57,
   59–60, 63, 82, 88
Hargrove, Sydney, 48–49
hate crimes, 7, 43–50, 51
Hate Crimes Prevention Act,
   46
HB-2, 9–10, 19–23, 26
health insurance, 7, 29–37, 72
hiring, 71
Hobby Lobby decision, 23
hormone level tests, 38, 41–42
hormones, 30–31, 33, 36, 38,

41–42, 66, 82
hormone therapy, 31, 66, 82
HRC Foundation, 60
Hudson, Tara, 88
Human Rights Campaign, 51

I
identity politics, 26–28
incarceration, 27, 43, 45,
   48–49, 54, 86–90
International Olympic
   Committee (IOC), 38,
   41–42
intersex people, 42, 46

J
Jim Crow, 26
job discrimination, 51, 54–55

K
Kalra, Anand, 32–33
Kennedy, Aydin, 30

L
Law, Victoria, 43
law enforcement, 27, 46–47,
   49–51, 53–56, 85
Liberty Counsel, 12
Lindner, Katharina, 38
Lopez, German, 79
Lynch, Loretta, 25

M
marriage rights, 5–7, 11, 23,
   72
Maryland State Education

PICTURE CREDITS